Caspar Schwenckfeld von Ossig
and the Ecumenical Ideal

by

Jack R. Rothenberger

B. S., B. D., S. T. M.

Published by
The Board of Publication of the Schwenkfelder Church
Pennsburg, Pennsylvania
1967

Copyright 1967
Library of Congress
Catalog Card Number: 67-31759

Printed in Germany by Hubert & Co., Göttingen
1967

Dedicated to the memory
of
HARVEY K. HEEBNER
(1877—1963)
Pastor of the First Schwenkfelder Church
of Philadelphia
(1906—1963)
and
for more than forty years
Editor of THE SCHWENKFELDIAN
a periodical published by the
Board of Publication
of the Schwenkfelder Church

We desire nothing more highly and pray for nothing more ardently than that the name of God and of Jesus Christ our Redeemer alone be praised and extolled with a sincere and genuine worship, and that His divine Word be proclaimed to all troubled souls in the whole world for their comfort.

CASPAR SCHWENCKFELD VON OSSIG

PREFACE

*I*t shall be the purpose of this thesis to show the type of Christian Caspar Schwenckfeld was, to relate him to some of the intellectual-spiritual movements of history, to locate the dominant concerns of this great Reformer, and to reveal clearly the impossibility of classifying Schwenckfeld neatly into a pigeon-hole. It is hoped that as a result of this study we shall be able to see how closely his ideas and goals seem to be synonymous with present expressions of the ecumenical ideal and to point in the direction The Schwenkfelder Church should move in the future.

At the 400th Anniversary Service commemorating the death of Schwenckfeld, December 10, 1961 in the Central Schwenkfelder Church, Dr. George H. Williams, Winn professor of ecclesiastical history and head of the church history department in the Harvard Divinity School, said of Schwenckfeld:

> This irenic nobleman of Silesia ... was almost unique among the reformers in having chosen to remain a layman, a layman in whose mind and heart were the seed of great fruitfulness ... in his vision of the universal church, (he) was clearly the heir of a great and richly complex tradition—classical, biblical, patristic, mystical. His was the vision of a universal church embracing the righteous faithful in all climes and times; his was the vision of the universal, peaceloving, serving and saving church of the ever-reigning Christ, the King of Grace.[1]

History is always a matter of interpretation. It is not an exact science but is conditioned by our various convictions and commitments. By careful selection, emphasis and continuous explanation the bare events of time are given meaning and purpose. What has been written about Caspar Schwenckfeld von Ossig, the Silesian nobleman who became a lay evangelist for the cause of Christ, is a clear illustration of the power of

---

[1] *The Schwenkfeldian*, November-December, 1961, p. 3.

VII

the historian's pen. Too often in the past church historians have been content to write off Schwenckfeld as a crack-pot or at least a threat to the *status quo*. However, today more and more scholars are concerning themselves with the life and teaching of this great man of the Protestant Reformation.

Obviously there is much work to be done in this area of study. Joachim Wach[2] says: ". . . such work will be appreciated by those willing to acknowledge greatness of character, profundity of thought, and true missionary zeal for Christ . . ." The writer is convinced the time has come for a broader view and a deeper understanding of the place Schwenckfeld occupies in the history of Christian thought. Furthermore, he is certain that such a view and understanding will add a considerable amount of constructive material necessary in the present attempts at reforming the church. The two basic marks of his thought—rejection of static orthodoxy and the experiential-experimental religious inwardness that expresses itself in all relationships of life—have still to be accomplished by the ecumenical church of today and tomorrow.

The writer wishes to take this opportunity to express his sincere gratitude to the following who have had much to do with his own Christian life and his understanding of Schwenckfeld's interpretation of the religion Jesus gave to man. First, to his Parents for providing a Christian home in which the importance of living one's beliefs was stressed. Second, to his wife Jean who, although his ancestors came over on the St. Andrew, introduced him to the Schwenkfelder Church while they were both teenagers. Third, to the late Dr. Elmer Ellsworth Schultz Johnson who was his teacher, friend and colleague, for giving him his first real knowledge of Schwenckfeld and for guidance in the first years as a Schwenkfelder minister. Fourth, to Dr. Selina G. Schultz who is the present authority on Schwenkfeldiana, for her suggestion of this theme, her helpful bibliography and her translations, without which this thesis could not have been written. Fifth, to the congregation of the Lansdale Schwenkfelder Church for being so patient as he was about this task instead of visiting in their homes. Sixth, to a host of professors at Juniata College, Hartford Theological Seminary and Temple University who have challenged and inspired him to seek the unity of the Church and to

---

[2] Jochim Wach, *Types of Religious Experience: Christian and Non-Christian,* (Chicago: University of Chicago Press, 1951), p. 135.

VIII

find an experiential-spiritual religion for his own life. Out of many more, these at least must be mentioned by name: Dr. G. Wayne Glick who had most to do with his decision to become a minister, Dr. Harvey K. MacArthur, Dr. Alexander C. Purdy, Dr. William Bradley, Dr. George Riggan, Dr. Matthew Spinka, Dr. Ford L. Battles, Dr. Moses Bailey and Dr. F. Ernest Stoeffler who seems to have gathered up his past Christian learning into a real grasp of the meaning of the experiential tradition. Seventh, to his fellow Schwenkfelder ministers who examined him and found him acceptable to become a licensed Schwenkfelder minister August 14, 1954: Harvey K. Heebner, Levi S. Hoffman, Robert J. Gottschall, Lester K. Kriebel, Dr. J. Maurice Hohlfeld, and Dr. Elmer E. S. Johnson. Finally, sincere appreciation to Mrs. Nevin Kelly, Jr. for typing and re-typing the manuscript for this thesis.

The following poem seems to sum up the search for the unity of Christ's Church in which Schwenckfeld was engaged. It is in the spirit of this poem that this study is presented.

Who Seeks Through Wastelands [3]
by Leslie Savage Clark

As one who searches deserts, dune on dune,
And finds but skulls and vulture wings, accursed
With loneliness and heat of blazing noon
So seeks the mind of man. How deep his thirst!
What alien countries, far and strange, his heart,
A prodigal, explores—to taste their wine,
And feasts one brief wild hour, till stripped, apart,
His hunger fain would share the husks with swine,
For these are restless things, the heart, the mind,
Whose old longings drive them east and west
Across the centuries until they find
The Living Water, Bread of Life, and rest.
For here alone is home, and man is stilled—
His thirsting quenched, his heart's long hunger filled.

---

[3] *The Christian Century*, January 19, 1955, p. 77 (reprinted by permission).

This thesis was originally submitted to the faculty in partial fulfilment of the requirements for the Degree of Master of Sacred Theology in the Graduate Program in Religion of Temple University 1962

CONTENTS

*Let no one allow his mind to be bound
by creeds and articles of faith that
he may not accept something better.*

CASPAR SCHWENCKFELD VON OSSIG

CHAPTER I

INTRODUCTION

1. Religion and Systematic Theology[4].

*R*eligion may be described as the way a person lives his life in relation to God and his fellow men. It involves living in the stream of the spirit[5] with an open mind and willing heart to receive the gift of God. After the gift is received, it involves relating personal faith to the world situation so that it is not merely a personal private thing. Thus, religion is not only a warm feeling or an emotional experience or an exercise of the mind. It is basically a matter of the inner experience of the soul expressing itself in day by day outer activity. As Walter Reif says: "The decisions Christians make daily where they live and do their work reveal the essence of their faith."[6]

Systematic theology, on the other hand, is a matter of the intellect. It is man's invention, his device to produce a correct doctrine about God and to develop precise details of faith, dogma, systems of doctrine, confessions of faith, creeds, etc., all of which are set forth to be accepted or rejected by others on the basis of a reasonable, or rational, proof. Systematic theology strives to be consistent and to remain within the bounds of logic as far as reason can take it. However, even in the most

---

[4] The writer is aware of the fact that the general concept of religion includes theology and cultic forms. However, for purposes of this thesis, in order to show Schwenckfeld's basic distinction between inner and outer religion, he makes a rather radical disjunction between religion (inner) and theology (outer). This concept of religion and systematic theology is derived from comments made by Dr. Selina G. Schultz in *A Course of Study in the Life and Teachings of Caspar Schwenckfeld von Ossig (1489—1561) and the History of the Schwenkfelder Religious Movement (1518—1958)*, (Pennsburg, Pa.: Board of Publication of the Schwenkfelder Church, 1959), pp. 136—137.

[5] Samuel M. Shoemaker, *With the Holy Spirit and With Fire*, (New York: Harper & Bros., 1960)

[6] *The Christian Century*, March 21, 1956.

logical theology there comes a point at which one must take the leap of faith. Most of the great Christian tenets cannot be proved absolutely. That is why we refer to the Christian Faith. It is "the assurance of things hoped for, the conviction of things not seen." Systematic theology is an attempt to interpret one's religious way of life so that one may have a reasonable faith.

The historic need for constant renewal of the church is due to the fact that from time to time institutionalized theology becomes dominant with its emphasis on right belief and neglects the necessity for a new life growing out of or based upon right belief. A careful study of history shows that whenever the flame of the institutional church burned low the Holy Spirit encouraged some to recall the church to its original emphasis upon the need for making one's belief evident in the way one lived his life.

Bishop Newbegin reminds us that those who cast emphasis upon the Holy Spirit and our need for his constant renewal in the church must be termed a necessary part of the whole church.[7] He says,

> Catholicism has laid its primary stress upon the given structure, Protestantism upon the given message... It is necessary, however, to recognize that there is a third stream of Christian tradition ... its central element is the conviction that the Christian life is a matter of the experienced power and presence of the Holy Spirit today; ... neither orthodoxy of doctrine nor impeccability of succession can take the place of this ... an excessive emphasis upon those immutable elements in the Gospel upon which orthodox Catholicism and Protestantism have concentrated attention may, and in fact often does, result in a Church which is a mere shell, having the form of a church but not the life; that if we would answer the question "Where is the Church?" we must ask "Where is the Holy Spirit recognizably present with power?"

To find "the Holy Spirit recognizably present with power" in the life of Christians was the purpose of Caspar Schwenckfeld von Ossig. He was a great man of religion who engaged in theological discussion in order to seek unity among all Christians. He expressed the ecumenical ideal in terms of a unity of purpose in the way Christians should live.

To know how Christians should live, Schwenckfeld raised questions about Christian beliefs. He wanted to discuss these questions with the other reformers of his day. He noted that when the mission and message of Jesus was studied and practiced by Christians they would necessarily

---

[7] Lesslie Newbegin, *The Household of God*, (New York: Friendship Press, 1954), pp. 94—95.

2

conclude that God may have other words for other worlds, but the Word of God for this world is Jesus himself. He formulated no system of doctrine that must be accepted in order to enter the Kingdom. To enter God's Kingdom men simply had to repent, change their minds, their ways, and obey God's command.

For Schwenckfeld, the Christian religion is personal response to the fact that . . . "In the beginning God"—and—"God so loved the world that He gave His only Son . . ." It is the response of our total selves to a God who is already acting on our behalf and whose will is expressed in terms of love.

This religion of response has no real need of striving, ceremony or mental acceptance of certain creedal formulations. God acts first. He comes to us in Jesus Christ. He is present today in the Holy Spirit. We don't search for him, we simply respond to him. Thus, Christian living is a reverent, grateful response to God as he made himself known in Jesus Christ. To love God means trusting him, obeying him, loving him, and loving those whom he loves.

When a person accepts Jesus as the Son of God, his own personal Savior, the Lord of all life, he becomes a Christian and begins living the Christian religion by the power of the indwelling Holy Spirit. Nothing he does by way of ritual observance or by way of good deeds or by way of repetition of certain creeds is enough to win the favor of God. God loves man so much that "while we were yet sinners" he gave his Son for us on the cross. Therefore, we cannot earn the right to be called Christian. We simply accept that right in humble faith. By accepting what God has done for us in Jesus Christ we unite with all others who name Jesus Lord, regardless of their race, nationality, or specific denomination. We thus become part of the family of God in the household of God—i.e., his Church.

Members of this household are marked by a peculiar characteristic known as love. They allow Christ to take charge of their lives and in a very literal sense the personality of Christ begins to possess them and show through them progressively as they grow in grace. *"No longer I live, but Christ liveth in me." "By this all men will know that you are my disciples, if you have love for one another."*

What is the Christian religion? Who is Jesus? According to Schwenckfeld we learn to know these things best by doing what he said, not by formulating creeds about him. Whoever really learns to know Jesus becomes a changed person.

A first step in knowing Jesus is to learn about the religion he brought to man. To learn about this religion, Schwenckfeld saw that we need to study the New Testament and after being thoroughly familiar with the New Testament we must study the Old Testament, the classics and the subsequent events of history in the light of the New Testament.

What we find in such a study is that a certain man named Jesus lived a life nearly two thousand years ago in Palestine. The people of his own day and the people ever since have interpreted his life and message and their interpretations have been, some true, some discolored, some false. Jesus never wrote anything. Why didn't he guard his mission and message against misinterpretation, faulty translation and inaccurate recording? Simply because he wanted to risk his message with people.

Christianity is not a book religion or a creed religion or a black and white religion and it never has been. Jesus' words and deeds have never been interpreted purely. Jesus threw his life right into the thick of life and faith and historical events in such a way that faith in him can never be completely expressed in words. The Gospel we preach is not in words but rather in the power of lives devoted to the cause of Christ. For Schwenckfeld the author of John seems to have really understood this when he said, "*the Word became flesh and dwelt among us.*" God entered into humanity in a very real way in Jesus.

In the New Testament we see life as it is and the impact of a supreme life on men as they were and are. The reality and vitality of Jesus and his work is brought out in a critical study of the New Testament. Schwenckfeld held that the New Testament itself is a response of faith to historical fact. Therefore, men have the right and the obligation to raise and attempt to answer searching questions about their faith and particular creeds. He claimed that the event of Christ in history gives men knowledge of God and gives them a way of approach to God, a way of living with God and an appreciation of the fact that all life comes from God. Because of the impact of Jesus' life upon his followers, they have refused to reduce him to a code of morals or a system of ideas or a theological creed. Therefore, in the interest of Christian unity, Schwenckfeld did not want to establish a formal creed.

4

The idea of Christ is not enough for Schwenckfeld. It is not enough to have a precise theology about him. There must be the fact of Christ, incarnate in our own lives. The Christian Gospel affirms that the supreme calamity of man is to be a man without a close relationship to God. Such a relationship enlarges one's life. It was and is the impact of Jesus, risking his message in terms of life, with weak and sinful men such as ourselves, which has given us the Christian Faith today. There have been many interpreters of that Faith in history. Caspar Schwenckfeld von Ossig was one of them.

Schwenckfeld worked diligently for a transformation of individual life so that a truly religious reformation of the Church would result. He was convinced that Jesus delivered religion from outward ceremonial form and ivory tower correctness and made it something infinitely simple, individual and inward. He put the accent upon simplicity as the best outward adornment for the spirit[8]. He said that the end of grace is to make a man essentially better and to make that betterment tell upon his neighbor's welfare. [9]

This kind of religion is not anything that is studied in books or in seminaries, but is the direct working of the Holy Spirit in the hearts of believers and this inner working shows increasingly in outward behavior. Schwenckfeld saw that Jesus dethroned the theologians of his time and preached not as the learned but as one who was inspired. He said "the official Christian and the nominal religionist alike are to be judged wholly by their conduct. No clothes . . . or external affectation . . . and no magic and no custom can help them. Everyone is on the dead level of equality (before God). The only questions are how do you think, how do you behave?" [10]

In order to understand his basic approach to religion, we note how Schwenckfeld always distinguished between the inner and outer in all things. This dualism must be kept in mind when reading his works[11]. He presupposes in his thinking a cosmological, ontological, philosophical and psychological dualism which dichotomizes the universe into the internal and external, the spiritual and material, the divine and creaturely. This

---

[8] *Corpus Schwenckfeldianorum*, (19 vols.; Leipzig: Breitkopf and Härtel, 1907—1961), I, xxxii. Cited hereafter as CS.

[9] *Ibid.*, p. xxxvi. [10] *Ibid.*, p. xxxvii.

[11] for example: *CS.*, II, 307, 354 ff, 404, 468, 485; III, 113, 176; IV, 549; V, 66—69; VIII, 188; IX, 113; X, 292; XV, 12—15.

fundamental distinction, which he probably learned from Tauler and a Neo-Platonism filtered through Patristic writings, can be observed in nearly every doctrine with which he concerned himself. [12]

Yet he did not arrive at the extremes of radical spiritualism or the errors of Gnosticism to which such ideas would theoretically lead. In practice he was not an enthusiast or *Schwärmer* as Luther said he was, and although he is often classed with them by others, Schwenckfeld acknowledged no kinship with them. In fact, he censured Franck, Bünderlin and others for completely ignoring all externals in their concern for the inner Word and Spirit. [13] Also, one of his major objections to the Anabaptists was their wholesale enthusiastic position, their legalism and their literal interpretation of scripture. He insisted that spiritual benefits are mediated independently of external observance whether it be the Lord's Supper, baptism, preaching, the church, etc., etc. He said the outer celebration or observance or practice has meaning only when the inner has taken place first, or at least simultaneously. [14]

In a recent study of Schwenckfeld, Paul Maier says: "The shunning of the external and the quest for the internal was Schwenckfeld's lot, his mission and his glory." [15] To this we hasten to repeat that Schwenckfeld did not neglect the external side of religion in his life. He would be one of the first to agree with Hugh Black who said: "True religion has always an eye to the practical. We should be suspicious of the piety which does not know service, of the prayers which do not lead to work, of the mysticism which begins and ends its own emotions." To be sure, Schwenckfeld's religion can be called a Christ-mysticism similar to that of the author of the Gospel of John and of that of the Apostle Paul for, like them, he always had an eye to the practical, too.

To sum up this section on religion and systematic theology, there are three basic affirmations of the Christian Faith which seem to be central to the religion of Jesus as interpreted by Caspar Schwenckfeld von Ossig.

1) Man has one and only one true object of worship. One holy God who is creator of all, lord of life, and redeemer of the repentant sinner. To commit life to him is to refuse to have any other gods at all.

---

[12] Paul L. Maier, *Caspar Schwenckfeld on the Person and Work of Christ,* (The Netherlands: Royal Van Gorcum Ltd. Assen., 1959).

[13] *CS.*, VII, 152.   [14] *Ibid.*, V, 170.

[15] Maier, *op. cit.*, p. 110.

2) Man is made for God. He can choose to accept God or to reject him. But in his limited freedom man also has creative power and destructive power. He has personal worth to God and God wants him to be the bearer of the high good at which the whole creation aims. Therefore, God revealed himself in human life in Jesus Christ and offers himself to man. But man is his own worst enemy and the greatest threat to the realization of the highest good comes from man himself for he is a fallen creature, *i.e.*, a sinner. He uses his limited freedom to set something other than the best at the center of his life and gives his allegiance to that. This is sin—*i.e.*, self at center.

3) God makes possible a new life for sinful man. God enables man to walk with faith, love and hope in true unlimited freedom. The way to this life is through personal surrender to Christ. This new life "in Christ" leads to a new community—the living Church. Christianity gives man true community with God and with his fellow men. But this can come, not through man's effort, not through imputation or ceremonial-creedal correctness, but only through a discovery that God, through his own forgiving love, does bring man into a sane, humble and personally creative relationship within the ecumenical church. To know God in Jesus Christ is the most necessary thing in life. To know him is to worship him. To worship him is to love him and to love him is to do his will as he gives the power and courage to obey. This is the Christian religion according to Schwenckfeld. Discussions, theories and creeds about this religion is called systematic theology.

2. The Experiential-Spiritual Religion of Schwenckfeld

For four hundred years Caspar Schwenckfeld has been largely hidden behind persecution, slander, misunderstanding, ignorance and fear. Until recently very few even heard of him and fewer made a thorough study of him or his ideas. Most good things written about Schwenckfeld were written by Schwenkfelder people themselves.

Today, with the increase of interest in the ecumenical church, experiential Christianity and the publication of the final volume of the *Corpus Schwenckfeldianorum*, more scholars are studying the facts of his life and ministry.

The misunderstandings began in 1526 when Luther, at the instigation of Melancthon, had little good to say about Schwenckfeld because he saw how his ideas would have disrupted the organizational structure of the institutional church. Schwenckfeld never became despondent over such misunderstandings. He knew that man's struggle for truth and community in freedom is not easy when he said: "After so many centuries of error we cannot expect to correct everything in a few short years." [16] Schwenckfeld had a profound hope that perhaps his religious ideas would be of service to another age. Today this hope is coming true.

The world situation today seems to be calling for a revival of Pietism in some modern form. As more research is being undertaken in this area of experimental-spiritual tradition of the Church we are finding that this "stream of the spirit" [17] goes back through the Gospel of John, the Apostle Paul to Jesus himself. Along with the Lutheran, Calvinistic, Anglican, Roman and Eastern traditions, this experiential-spiritual tradition is being recognized as a worthy field of study. To be sure, it is the channel uniting the whole history of Christianity. Caspar Schwenckfeld von Ossig is a major participant in this particular stream.

The basic characteristics of this type of Christianity are (1) individual relationship to God, (2) religious idealism holding the goal of spiritual perfection as possible for the spirit-filled individual and (3) strong emphasis on the biblical revelation with an openness to reason but with much emphasis upon ethical conduct based on one's relationship to God rather than emphasis on rites and ceremonies and creeds.

Research into this area of Christian thought is showing that the Pietistic or experiential-spiritual tradition cannot be limited to the seventeenth and eighteenth centuries. Schwenckfeld is inevitably assigned to the left wing of the Reformation [18] because this is the great catch-all for independent thinkers of that era. He was not oriented toward Rome, Wittenberg, Zurich or Geneva. And though he shared some aspects of the Anabaptists, other spirituals, the mystics and "anti-trinitarian" rationalists such as dissatisfaction with the morals of those within the Reformation churches and opposition to established or folk churches—both Roman

---

[16] S. Schultz, *Course of Study* ..., p. 8.
[17] Shoemaker, *op. cit.*
[18] Rufus M. Jones, *Spiritual Reformers in the 16th and 17th Centuries,* (Boston: Beacon Press, 1914).

Catholic and Protestant—he was unlike them in many other respects. For this reason, Dr. Paul Maier[19] says it is better to speak of Schwenckfeld as one of the side-currents of the Reformation rather than as definitely a part of the left wing.

However, in searching for middle ground between Wittenberg and the Anabaptists, he found the Lutheran means of grace the worst evil and thus tended to lean in the direction of the left by saying externals are of secondary importance to the Christian. Dr. Selina Schultz[20] claims the principles of Schwenckfeld give incentive and impetus to later parallel movements such as Pietism, Quakerism, Methodism, the Separatists of England and the German Apostolic Church movement. "His religious ideas, although generally unknown or unrecognized, are living on in modern religious thought."[21]

Many authorities have designated Schwenckfeld as the "fountainhead of Pietism" a "Pietist before Pietism" and its parallels. Joachim Wach[22] says of him: "There can be no doubt that Caspar Schwenckfeld von Ossig is one of the worthiest and most attractive figures in the era of the Reformation—nay, in the history of Christianity—and that the attention which has been given to his person and his work is in reverse proportion to their importance."

An unidentified sixteenth century writer says: "An arch-heretic, if one asks his enemies; and a saint, if one reads him himself."[23]

> Among all the reformers of the sixteenth century who worked at the immense task of recovering, purifying and restating the Christian faith, no one was nobler in life and personality and no one was more uncompromisingly dedicated to the mission of bringing into the life of the people a type of Christianity winnowed clean from the husks of superstition and tradition grounded in ethical and spiritual reality than was Schwenckfeld, the Silesian noble. No one to a greater degree than he succeeded in going behind not only Scholastic formulations, but even behind Pauline interpretations of Christ, to Christ himself.[24]

---

[19] Paul L. Maier, "Caspar Schwenckfeld and the Schwenckfelders," address to the 76th Annual Meeting of the American Historical Association, December 29—30, 1961 at Washington, D. C.

[20] Schwenkfelder historian, editor of the CS. and author of the only Biography of Schwenckfeld.

[21] S. Schultz, *Caspar Schwenckfeld von Ossig: Spiritual Interpreter of Christianity, Apostle of the Middle Way, Pioneer in Modern Religious Thought.* (Philadelphia: Walther Printing House, 1947), p. 400.

[22] Wach, *op. cit.,* p. 135.

[23] CS., XI, 80.   [24] Jones, *op. cit.,* p. 64.

If we must classify Schwenckfeld, we might agree with Paul Maier when he calls him an "Evangelical Spiritualist" as contrasted with the "Revolutionary Spiritualist" of the *Schwärmer* or Sebastian Franck's "Rational Spiritualism."[25] He was evangelical in a Johannine sense with traces of patristic Neo-Platonism and mysticism as found in Tauler. Dr. Maier correctly refers to Schwenckfeld as the "Irenaeus of the Reformation" for he preached Eastern soteriology in the West and was constantly seeking Christian unity.

Schwenckfeld's pen became his pulpit after he was deprived of the use of the pulpits of Southern Germany and as a result he produced more than 1,250 pieces of literary works. One hundred and eighty—five of these are books and booklets. Many of them are similer to later Pietistic devotional literature.

Like the later Pietists he considered meditation as a first and indispensable step in the search for truth. It was his constant daily custom to write and study early in the day and late at night, reading at least four chapters from the Bible each day. He believed that prayer and study were of central importance to Christian growth. He claimed "a little read daily with understanding is better than much with lack of it, or without reflection and attentiveness."[26] He practiced such personal study faithfully even upon his death-bed.[27] In the *Corpus Schwenckfeldianorum*[28] he gives suggestions for meditation for each day of the week. His devotional books have been called the best of the Reformation Century,[29] and they reveal the beauty and depth of his spiritual life and thought.

Of all the books of Schwenckfeld the book of prayers, *Passional*, was the most widely circulated and read.[30] "There is hardly one devotional book of the 18th century more pietistic than this prayer book of 1539 which, if its origin had remained undisclosed, would certainly be classified

---

[25] These categories were first suggested by Dr. George H. Williams in his book *Spiritual and Anabaptist Writers*, p. 31 ff., as quoted in Dr. Maier's address Dec., 1961.

[26] Wach, *op. cit.*, p. 147.

[27] Christopher Schultz, *A Vindication of Caspar Schwenckfeld von Ossig*, trans. and ed., Elmer Schultz Gerhard, (Allentown, Pa.: Schlechter, 1942), pp. 311—319.

[28] *CS.*, XII, 714.

[29] Paul Althaus, *Zur Charakteristik der evangelischen Gebetslitteratur im Reformations-jahrhundert*, (Leipzig: 1914), p. 252.

[30] This has been translated from *CS.*, VI, 651f. in 1961 in connection with the 400th Anniversary of the death of Caspar Schwenckfeld by John Joseph Stoudt and published by the Schwenkfelder Library.

as a typical 18th century product, again proof for the opinion that Schwenckfeld was rightly called a 'Pietist before Pietism.' " [31]

The Pietism which Schwenckfeld lived and taught was of a high standard, void of visionary fanaticism and enthusiastic outbursts.[32] His "Middle Way" appears to be the maturist part of the sixteenth century Reformation in spite of the fact that Luther branded him as visionary and fanatical. Beginning in 1524 the main stream of the reformatory movements were sinking back into a one-sided orthodoxy from which Schwenckfeld was repelled.

We cannot measure the importance of Schwenckfeld's experiential-spiritual religion by counting the number of Schwenckfelders today. It is not a matter of quantity but of quality and depth. Schwenckfeld himself refused to found a new church, nevertheless as a lay preacher he held private devotional services and drew into his circle pious, learned men with whom he sought to build a real inward Christianity. For a time he succeeded in winning large communities to a deeper spirituality by his pastoral care and sincerity of purpose. Through the conventicle method many leaders of the church and the state were convinced of the rightness of his reformation activity. "These Schwenckfeldian pietistic groups formed the groundwork for the pietistic movement of the seventeenth century, which also played an important part in the development of freedom of faith." [33]

It is very difficult to determine who influenced whom in this Reformation Era, but we can safely say that Schwenckfeld made a significant impact on a fairly broad spectrum of people ranging from radicals like Franck and Hoffman to moderates like Zell and Capito, to such princes as Philip of Hesse and Joachim II of Brandenburg. His precise influence in particular areas needs to be explored but his courageous defense of the persecuted, his consistent views on full religious liberty and freedom of conscience, his desire for Christian unity, all came to the fore in a later more tolerant age.

Dr. Maier suggests that the most traceable current of Schwenckfeld's influence is in "Spiritualistic Christianity" which is expressed in warm,

---

[31] Robert Friedmann, *Mennonite Piety Through the Centuries,* (Goshen: 1949), pp. 5, 193.

[32] S. Schultz, *Caspar Schwenckfeld . . .*, pp. 400—407.

[33] *Ibid.,* p. 403.

personal, inner faith that shows in practical life. "Probably Johann Arndt, and definitely Valentine Weigel and Jacob Boehme read much of Schwenckfeld. Spenner came from the Schwenckfelder community of Rappoltsweiler, and Pietism flourished especially in the areas where Schwenckfeld had been most active—Lutheran orthodoxy often looked upon Pietism as 'reborn Schwenckfeldianism.'—Schwenckfeld's teachings migrated and (most likely) considerably influenced English Quakerism and Congregationalism."[34]

It is very unlikely that any of the "major Reformers" understood Schwenckfeld in their day but as Troeltsch indicated[35] he was "the leader, or at least the type" of most of the spiritual reformers who arrived "... to breathe new life into the Christian movement, and to make it active and effective ..." In Schwenckfeld's opinion, established Protestantism had too quickly assumed the authoritarian position of Rome and had become a dry orthodoxy.

It seems quite clear that Schwenckfeld was in the pietistic stream before Pietism evolved as a specific part of the Protestant Reformation. Like the later Pietists, he emphasized the necessity of growing in faith daily by the direct influence of the Holy Spirit. Like them, he emphasized the work of the Holy Spirit and the need for freedom to continue the reformation endlessly in personal experience in order to make one's religion practical. Like them he was biblically oriented. At all times his guiding motivation lay in the area of practical Christianity.[36]

Sick at heart because of the divisions arising within Christ's Church he endeavored to emphasize a warm, personal Christianity based upon direct encounter with God, true to the message of the Bible, which involved an entire change in a person so that the unity of Christ's body might be maintained from within. His primary purpose to which his whole life and his every effort in thinking, writing and teaching were dedicated was the service of Christ. He wanted to build a personal Christianity in individual lives, believing that a genuinely free, united Christian Church would evolve as a consequence.

---

[34] Maier, "Caspar Schwenckfeld ..." address. also CS. Biog. p. 401—410.
[35] *Social Teaching*, as quoted by Maier, *Ibid.*, p. 751.
[36] Maier, *op. cit.*, p. 9.

CHAPTER II

HIS LIFE AND TIMES

1. Age of Reformation

*C*aspar Schwenckfeld was very sensitive to note the condition which existed around him. He knew the time was ripe for finding life's meaning in a new kind of world that was coming to be in the sixteenth century. It was the age of new birth in all areas of life.

It was an age of fundamental change in outlook due to an increasing sense of history and historical perspective. Primarily, it was an age characterized by a break from the medieval other worldly view to an interest in this world. There were many deep-lying tendencies away from the bondage and traditions of the past. Tendencies such as (1) A desire for economic and social reforms to liberate the common people and give them a chance to become real persons. (2) A vast undercurrent moving toward intellectual, spiritual and social freedom. (3) A deep "yearning among serious people for a religion of inward experience . . . based not on proof-texts nor on external authority of any kind, but on the native capacity of the soul to seek, to find and to enjoy the living God who is the Root and Sap of every twig and branch of the great tree of life." [37]

New life, new hopes, new desires, as well as new fears and anxieties were to be found everywhere. Progress in every direction except in the Roman Catholic Church. The medieval church wielded a power beyond the dreams of any secular monarch. But, if any power or any institution is to endure, it must be progressive. The real tragedy of the Roman Church of the sixteenth century is that it failed to move with the times. Here was stagnation, obscurantism, and corruption.

---

[37] Jones, *op. cit.*, p. 3.

Reformation of the church became an absolute necessity because it did not serve adequately the deep religious needs of the people of that new age. The basic question in the minds and hearts of the people was: How can I be saved? The church, instead of showing them the way, was the largest part of their bondage. The church itself needed saving. It needed inner reform.

The reforming movement achieved a measure of success in its first years because it came when the hearts and minds of men were stirred with deep-seated yearnings in all areas of life. A long period of preparation, including various attempts at inner reform, preceded 1517. The big question then was, "could the church reform itself from within or must there be a new start?"

This writer agrees with Rufus Jones when he says, "one of the greatest tragedies in Christian history is the division of forces which occurred in the reformation movements of the sixteenth century."[38] As we look back on this period of history, we can see the necessity, the how and why of these divisions. Nevertheless, they are still tragic: perhaps the time has come today for achieving the real purpose of the reformers as revealed in that period of history from 1517 to 1523 which was characterized by a spirit of unity among the liberating forces. Caspar Schwenckfeld apparently continued in that spirit throughout his life. He was not long in detecting after 1523, and much to his sorrow, aspects of weakness in the new type of Christianity which was spreading over Germany. In 1524 he called attention to the superficiality of the change which was taking place in men's lives as a result of the Reformation. He approved of Luther's central principles but pointed out that little will be gained if they are adopted only on the intellectual level and held as a new "orthodoxy" in authoritarian ways.[39]

2. Early Life—Education—Awakening

Caspar Schwenckfeld von Ossig was born in the district of Lüben in the duchy of Liegnitz, Lower Silesia (Eastern Germany today), to an

---

[38] *Ibid.,* p. 1 ff.

[39] "An Admonition to the Brethren of Silesia," *CS.,* II, 26—105. This letter indicates how clearly Schwenckfeld understood his age and shows how he intended to meet the real need of his day.

ancient noble family who had given distinguished service in the political and ecclesiastical life of that country for many years. His parents, Hans von Schwenckfeld and Barbara von Kreckwitz, came from prolific, wealthy and influential stock and it is from such a background the young Caspar received much cultural and spiritual influences which helped to form his character.

His pious Christian parents had him baptized in infancy and reared him in the Roman Catholic faith. Caspar had a brother named Hans and a sister whose name is not known. As he grew to manhood, his stately appearance, his dignified behavior, sharp honesty, modesty, kindness, piety and gentleness in dealing with everyone won him the respect of most people who knew him. His youth was lived in and about the castle home of his parents at Ossig in a picturesque rural setting. Throughout his life he held dear the memory of his family and homeland.

Caspar never married. After the death of his father, his brother and he inherited the large estate at Ossig in 1519. It seems he also owned, perhaps in partnership with Hans, an estate at Wohlau. [40] It was from these large holdings that Caspar received an income through life enabling him to live independently and in voluntary exile for thirty-two years.

Dr. Seyppel points out that when Caspar was just about to leave the lap of his family the young Martin Luther, in 1505, entered the Augustinian Monastery of Erfurt. Caspar's student days have not been recorded very accurately. However, it is known that he attended several universities, mention being made that he studied in Cologne for two years, 1505—1507, and matriculated at the University of Frankfurt on the Oder in 1507. His knowledge of Latin, the classics and the Church Fathers, his elegant style as a writer and his vocabulary show that he received the thorough preparatory training which was customary at that time and his works give evidence of excellent training and scholarship. His period of systematic study ended around 1511. From 1511 to 1521 he was an adviser to three dukes of Silesia. This period was a type of school for him too. He referred frequently to his experiences in highly honorable positions. [41] He refers also to the evils and hypocrisies of court life in that day. In addition he became a knight of the Teutonic Order. [42] By 1523

---

[40] CS., II, 145, 608.
[41] Ibid., IV, 789; V, 535; VI, 489—490; VII, 44; XIV, 47.
[42] Ibid., I, 269; VII, 237.

15

his hearing became so badly impaired that he had to give up his very active career in the service of the courts. He returned to Ossig but continued as an occasional adviser to his personal friend, Duke Frederick II of Liegnitz.

The first news of what Luther did at Wittenberg in 1517 reached Silesia in 1518. Caspar's attention was immediately and profoundly attracted by Luther's *Letter to the German Nobility*. His first spiritual awakening can be dated in the year 1518. He frequently referred to his awakening and said he was called by God away from court life where he had lived sinfully [43] and that he was given spiritual gifts to the praise of God and the benefit of mankind. [44] At once he began a thorough study of the Scriptures, the Church Fathers, and all the writings coming from the pens of the leaders of the Reformation.

Caspar always remembered it was Luther who called him to an awakening and held Luther in high regard all his life. He was himself a Lutheran for eight years. In 1526, Caspar had another "spiritual awakening" or "mystical experience" which was the breakthrough of his own peculiar ideas concerning the Lord's Supper. "From that time on he recognized that he could no longer spiritually follow any man." [45] He no longer traveled the common, easy road but went into the thicket of a mystical-spiritual religion with "ancient roots and future branches."

3. The Silesian Reformation

By 1522 Caspar had won the Duke of Liegnitz and many of the educated leaders of Silesia to support of the Reformation. He had become the author of the Silesian Reformation. He advocated patient instruction of the ignorant and superstitious masses as well as of the clergy because he was convinced the change in the church must come from within if it is to be lasting and if it is to become truly an ecumenical church. As a lay preacher he devoted his efforts first of all to his own community.

After being an ardent Lutheran for eight years, in 1526 Schwenckfeld began to think of Luther as the greatest enemy of a "personal experiential

---

[43] *Ibid.,* VI, 609; IX, 60 f., 421; XI, 583; XII, 133.

[44] *Ibid.,* IV, 775 f.; XIV, 236.

[45] Joachim H. Seyppel, *Schwenckfeld: Knight of Faith,* (Pennsburg, Pa.: The Schwenkfelder Library, 1961), p. 30. also see CS. Biog. p. 100 ff.

Christianity." The rift between Luther and Schwenckfeld occurred when Luther's growing sacramentalism could not be reconciled by Schwenckfeld to the New Testament teaching on the subject of the sacraments. Either salvation is by faith or it is by the sacraments—not both, Schwenckfeld said. Of course, he sided with faith and claimed Luther was becoming too much of a sacramentarian, i.e., putting too much value on the elements and the outward ceremony.

Along these same lines, Schwenckfeld said that the idea of a mass institutional church is a medieval idea, not Biblical. The true Church is not constituted by preaching and sacraments, not the gathering together of a large assembly of people, but by the presence of the Holy Spirit. The outward marks of the Church are the fruits of the Spirit such as communion of saints, knowledge of Christ, true faith in God, patience, fear of God, unity of spirit, etc. Schwenckfeld charged that the Lutheran church of his day had done little to change the lives of the people in an ethical way and therefore he would change from what he called a "head faith" to a "heart faith." He wanted a religion that changed the lives of its people.

This occurred in 1526. It was the beginning of the "Middle Way" for a group of people who were to become known as Schwenckfelders. Schwenckfeld said that this new light was an act of conscious surrender to God and an awareness of God's acceptance of him through the redemptive work of Christ alone.

Schwenckfeld said that the literalism and externalism of Luther was leading to greater divisions among Christians. He noted that the reformation churches were making little change in the lives of church members. He and Luther entered into open debate and in 1528 Schwenckfeld wrote his Duke saying: "Luther led us out of Egypt, through the Red Sea into the wilderness, and has left us to wander there in untrodden paths, trying to persuade us that we are already in the promised land." [46]

Schwenckfeld was determined to follow Christ, the Middle Way as he called it, to the Kingdom of God. He formulated no creed, or system of doctrine, sought no following, and refused to form a distinct denomination, believing that such a step would cause separation from others and prevent him from being of service to all. He considered spiritual life

---

[46] CS., III, 105.

17

and experience of far greater importance than creeds, dogmas and learned theologies. If a name had to be given to those who agreed with him he wanted them to be called: "Confessors of the Glory of Christ." He based his teachings on the Scriptures, interpreted spiritually, not literally, and particularly on the Gospel of John. His motto was "Nil Triste, Christo Recepto—Wenn ich Christum habe, bin ich nicht traurig." "When I have Christ I am not sad."

This became the banner of the Silesian Reformation. Wolfgang Knorrlich[47] claims that without Schwenckfeld's activity in the early years the reformation in Silesia would have remained a dead issue. His evangelistic activity devoted to the glory of God, the proclamation of the word of God, and the winning of the individual for the Gospel and for exemplary living were not only the heart and soul of the evangelical movement in Silesia but are still representative of an ecumenical mission in the world today. The moderness of Schwenckfeld's aims appears in his tolerance, his insistence upon freedom of conscience, separation of church and state and upon Christian living. This was the nature of the Silesian reformation which was carried out primarily through the conventicle method. He had the support of the people and the dukes. Gradually large opposition arose from the clergy on both sides, the Lutheran and the Roman.

On many occasions and for various reasons Schwenckfeld set forth his confession of faith for many eminent and common persons alike. These can be found and read in the *Corpus Schwenckfeldianorum*. One such statement begins:[48]

> I hope and trust in God that I have by means of His divine grace given my answer and confession concerning the Holy Sacrament of the blood and body of Jesus Christ quite frankly and Christlike, according to the evidences of Holy Scriptures... I know not whereon to base my Christian belief except on God the Father Almighty, maker of heaven and earth (Genesis 1) and on Jesus Christ our Lord who is the Word, the Wisdom and the only begotten natural and eternal Son of God the Father, through whom and by whom all things were made, set in operation, controlled and maintained; (John 1; Romans 11) who for our sake was made man. Since man alone of all creatures fell out of the order and obedience to God, he took flesh upon Himself that He might condemn sin in

---

[47] S. Schultz, "A Review of Dr. Knorrlich's dissertation presented to the Philosophical Faculty of the University of Bonn for his PhD.," *The Schwenkfeldian*, Vol. 55, no. 5 (September-October, 1958), p. 4 f.

[48] *CS.*, VIII, 231 ff.

the flesh (Romans 13; I Peter 2) purify our corrupt flesh, reconcile man with God and bring him back to life eternal. (Luke 19:2, 2 Corinthians 5) ... God came into flesh so that our flesh might come again into God.[49]

The true Church of Jesus Christ for Schwenckfeld is the company of God's people who are believers in Christ with heart, mind and soul. In his concept of the Church Schwenckfeld comes very close to the modern ecumenical ideal. Although he did not want to organize a church in his name, he endeavored to fulfill Christ's prayer "that they may be one." Schwenckfeld distinguished between the external and the spiritual church. He and his followers formed a pious *ecclesiola in ecclesia*. The spiritual Church can be found in every external church and therefore Schwenckfeld was ready to give his right hand of fellowship to any Romanist, Lutheran, Reformed, Anabaptist or whatever name given to a person, providing that the other believed in Christ and behaved like a Christian. His principle of unity was fraternity. "All Christians should be brothers first and last, however variant their theological explanations might be." He said, "I am most concerned that I be a member of the Church of God to which belong all those in all lands wherever they may be, who sincerely serve and worship God, whether or not they belong to any one confession of faith or order of worship."[50] He labored for a truly ecumenical church which was to come slowly by a gradual transformation of individual lives within the external churches. He believed that from transformed individuals a truly free Christian Church would evolve. He claimed that most of the dissensions in Christendom were due to the insistence upon the superficialities of religion and the literal interpretation of Scripture.

Christian unity, according to Schwenckfeld, cannot be built on compulsory adherence to man-made creeds and organizations, or on strained theological theories for the sake of peace. Christian unity can come through the knowledge of Christ and the spiritual interpretation of Scripture, on freedom of the individual to make his own decisions as he is moved by the Holy Spirit, on faith in Jesus Christ which gives one a free conscience. Of these fundamental principles there could be no compromise.

---

[49] The full content of this statement of faith cannot be given here but this is enough to see how Christocentric and Scriptural Schwenckfeld attempted to be.

[50] Schultz, *Course of Study ...*, p. 18.

Faith for the Silesian Reformer meant being aware of God's constant presence, fellowship with him, participation in the divine nature through Christ and the power of the Holy Spirit, and total dependence upon God in all things. As Schwenckfeld would not allow his conscience to be coerced so he refused to force anyone to accept his views. He claimed that the fundamental truths of the Christian religion must come to a person through the process of regeneration—which is the result of a personal experience and knowledge of the living Christ.

For Schwenckfeld, true worship of God "consists in loving God, and loving God means doing his will." It was and is a practical religion which expresses itself in sharing the burdens of all who are in need. In that sense, Schwenckfeld believed in the church as a "redemptive society" of sinners who having accepted God's forgiveness through Jesus Christ in its external form seeks to serve Christ by meeting the needs of others in love.

This was the nature of the Silesian Reformation:

4. Exile Years

> Had I desired a good place on earth, I would have remained in my fatherland, in my own house and castle where I had position as well as high regard, and was dear to the powerful of this world ... Had I desired to live selfishly and have the respect of men, I could have remained at home ... I left house and home and all that is dear to a man, for the sake of the Gospel of Christ.[51]

Although Caspar Schwenckfeld was not a controversialist by nature he was engaged in serious controversy with the learned reformers of his day. In 1528, Zwingli in Zurich was seeking sympathetic support for his Eucharistic views in his battle against Luther. He found a tractate on the Lord's Supper written by Schwenckfeld, Crautwald and others of Silesia and, noting its tone, decided to publish it as support for his own views.

Luther, already knowing Schwenckfeld's views concerning the Supper as a result of their conferences and verbal battles in 1525, at once became enraged about Zwingli's publication. Caspar had not given Zwingli permission to publish this booklet. Nevertheless, he went ahead and this

---

[51] *CS.*, IX, 651; VII, 44; VIII, 608; XV, 184.

resulted in much difficulty between Caspar and the Lutherans in his area.

Like Luther, Zwingli had mistakenly understood Schwenckfeld's views, thinking they were in agreement with his own. Because of this opposition, and because Caspar wanted to protect his Duke from political embarrassment, he left home and never returned. He traveled much in these years, remaining in a place as long as the heat of controversy permitted. Strassburg, that temporary haven for independent thinkers, Augsburg, Ulm and other cities were to be his home. He was never completely safe from those who differed from him.

Schwenckfeld arrived in Strassburg in 1529, where he met many important men, among them Paracelsus, Karlstadt, Sebastian Franck, Martin Bucer, Wolfgang Capito (in whose house Schwenckfeld stayed), Matthaeus Zell, other Swiss reformers, Anabaptists and people like Adam Reisner, Jacob Held von Tieffenau and Alexander Berner et. al. who were to become his most loyal followers. He enjoyed fruitful years in Strassburg because there was a genuine friendly interest in his teachings by the preachers of that city. The more sympathetic attitude of the South German and Swiss reformers in general aided him in gaining many adherents to his opposition to externalism and literalism. He attended church services to worship as well as to preach. He gave lectures and held religious disputations in conventicles constantly. He never attacked the institutional church as such, but he strongly opposed the externalism and superficiality into which the church had drifted. Like his brotherhoods in Liegnitz before his voluntary exile, those in Strassburg were very succesful and were for the purpose of worship, study and religious nurture patterned after the New Testament church practices.

Because of the compromising work of Martin Bucer, who became Caspar's arch enemy in spite of much similarity in basic convictions, many of the more liberal persons in Strassburg began leaving the "Middle Way." Zwingli's death in 1531 and Calvin's forced departure from France in 1533, plus a rising hatred for the Anabaptism in its more fanatical *Münster* forms in 1535, all combined to give the spiritual reformers cause for fear. It was because of Martin Bucer that Schwenckfeld was forced to leave Strassburg. However, as a result of Schwenckfeld's stay in the Strassburg-Landau-Speyer-Rappoltsweiler area, a strong Schwenckfeldian community existed for a century thereafter. The great

German Pietist, Jacob Philip Spener (1635—1705) lived and worked in this region.[52]

Both in Silesia and then in Strassburg Schwenckfeld had begun to build, by practical procedures, a better educated clergy of good moral character. He, Crautwald and others had established an "ecumenical university" in Liegnitz to create and keep peace and harmony through a better understanding among all religious parties. He had written the first catechism of the Reformation and used this method of instruction for young and old in his conventicles. The *ecclesiola in ecclesia* was basic to the new Christian life within the communities where his influence was felt. The *"stillstand"* or suspension of the practice of the Lord's Supper until the laity and clergy alike had received proper instruction regarding the value, significance and spiritual understanding of it became a kind of trademark of Schwenckfeld. He personally gave material aid to the poor peasants who suffered from economic and religious oppression by overbearing priests. The practice of believer's baptism (but not re-baptism or Anabaptism) as a sign of what has already taken place in the believer and the reformation of the monastery along evangelical lines—all of this as well as other practical measures were part of Schwenckfeld's reformation from within outward. These practices were gaining good results when down upon him came anathemas, mandates, misrepresentations and severe persecutions.[53] It was a very intolerant age when each group or each person in many cases felt they had all the truth and would not even listen to anyone else. Schwenckfeld, in spite of the age, was tolerant and willing to listen, discuss or debate any matter, but he would accept only what was acceptable to Scripture and what brought honor to God instead of to man or to a particular man.

In regard to Martin Bucer, Schwenckfeld became a hindrance to his schemes "to establish a fixed and uniform system of religious doctrine, a politico-ecclesiastical union against Rome, and to banish from the city all those who thought independently of that system and dared to say so."[54]

Bucer was always traveling in Germany, attending various councils, compromising here and there in order to form a united church that

---

[52] S. Schultz, *Caspar Schwenckfeld ...*, p. 177.
[53] *Ibid.*, p. 170.
[54] *Ibid.*, p. 196.

would have power to keep its control, whereas Schwenckfeld consistently urged leniency and kindness toward all.[55] Schwenckfeld constantly held that constraint of conscience makes hypocrites, not Christians. "In his estimation, there is nothing that will so embitter the human heart, cause discontent and discord as when one attempts to force another to his faith."[56] Patience, kindness and instruction in spiritual understanding of Scripture brings the knowledge of Christ which alone can give concord among Christians.

Because of their basic differences in approaching Christian unity, Dr. Selina Schultz claims that Martin Bucer is the origin of the opposition which met Schwenckfeld in every place he went in Southern Germany to the end of his days.[57]

These views forced him to leave his home when he came into conflict with the Lutherans. They now caused him to leave Strassburg in search of a new haven in 1533. For the rest of his days, Schwenckfeld lived in and near Ulm, in Swabia. The religious, mystic impulse of the Swabians proved to be congenial to the Silesian.[58] Three hundred years before, Tauler and Seuse had been active in this region.

He spent a year in Augsburg where some of the richest families of Europe lived. At the University of Tübingen[59] a colloquy between Schwenckfeld and several Protestant conformists was held in 1535, during which Caspar refused to acknowledge anyone as a Christian because he insisted that is a matter known only to God. He still insisted on the inward religion. However, a year later, 1536, the Lutheran Wittenburg Formula Concordiae brought orthodoxy its final victory in the movement for Christian Protestant concord, holding up the supremacy of the outward word.

It is interesting to note that the civil authorities, burgo-masters, secretaries of councils, councilmen and nobility admired Schwenckfeld and his views. But the clergy who, apparently jealous of his popularity, persisted in banishing him from their towns and cities. They usually resorted to half-truths, untruths and malicious rumor to make life diffi-

---

[55] CS., VI, 257—259, 832—836, also S. Schultz, op. cit., p. 204.
[56] Ibid., p. 178.   [57] Ibid., p. 219.
[58] Seyppel, op. cit., p. 35.
[59] Very active in Schwenckfelder research today, Selina G. Schultz received a D. theol. degree from here in 1961 for her life work as Schwenkfelder historian in America.

cult for Caspar. The power of Bucer and Blaurer's propaganda worked succesfully against him. They charged that Schwenckfeld was "a sectarian creating dissension in the church" that he was "misleading the people" and that "he was an Anabaptist."

After the Tübingen colloquy, there seems to have been a thaw in the attitude of Bucer to Schwenckfeld. Blaurer also seems to have been affected permanently by Schwenckfeld's sincerity, balanced approach, fraternal appeal and forceful example of practical Christianity.[60]

Nevertheless, the unionistic movement begun by Bucer in 1529 culminated, as pointed out above, in the victory of orthodoxy at the Wittenberg Concordia in 1536. By compromise, Bucer had surrendered his last point, that which had to do with the Lord's Supper.

It must be emphasized that Caspar Schwenckfeld was no less desirous than they for Christian unity. However, he believed such unity must be based upon freedom of conscience, knowledge of Christ, understanding, love and persuasion, not upon compromise arrived at by blind acceptance due to coercion. He criticised the Wittenberg Concordia very strongly, especially Articles II and III which had to do with Bucer's compromise with Luther on the Lord's Supper.

Everywhere Caspar went he contended for the rights and liberty of the laymen to think, to believe, to express, to discuss and to expound religious truths. The politico-ecclesiastical leaders considered this degrading to their own prestige. Also, because of Schwenckfeld, attendance in their church services was falling off while he attracted many to his conventicle meetings. This added to the threat of his safety wherever he went. He always offered to prove his beliefs and practices by Scriptural evidence and by the testimony of the Church Fathers, of the young Luther and of others but the authorities were growing more and more unwilling to listen to him.[61] Caspar's characteristic remark was, "Jesus and his disciples coerced no one. There can be no reason so great as to justify taking the life of anyone because of his religious ideas. The true Christian Church does not persecute."[62] It was not only the Roman Catholic Church, but also the Lutheran, the Calvin-Reformed and others who were using such methods of coercion. Schwenckfeld would not have that kind of unity.

---

[60] S. Schultz, *Caspar Schwenckfeld . . .*, p. 237.
[61] *CS.*, V, 340—341.
[62] S. Schultz, *Course of Study . . .*, p. 17.

During his five years in the city of Ulm (1534—1539) he became more and more interested in Christology and wrote much on this subject.[63] He maintained Christ was not a creature but a new, divine man, the Son of God, God and man in one person, the Lord eternal, coequal with God the Father from before the beginning of the world. Although proving his views by Scripture, the orthodox parties would not accept them. Furious denunciations again were passed against Caspar by the Schmalkald League in 1540, largely by the hand of Melanchthon. Rufus Jones says, "to his anti-Lutheran views on the sacraments he had now added teachings on the nature of Christ which the theologians pronounced unorthodox."[64]

During the Roman Counter-Reformation of Pope Paul III, the threat of the Jesuits from 1540 on, and the condemnations of Bucer and Melanchthon Schwenckfeld continued to write incessantly. His pen was his sole pulpit now. He wrote much, using many different pseudonyms in order to protect himself. For several years he hid in the Justingen Castle near Ulm until 1547. He made many secret journeys during this period, traveling in disguise and often in bad weather with little physical protection from the elements. In 1541 he wrote his great Confession of faith while hiding in the library of the Benedictines in Kempten.[65] Several years of Christological controversy followed between the Lutherans and Zwinglians against himself.

Throughout all these controversies he refused to become bitter, resentful or unreasonable but remained calm, and exercised intelligent, forceful reasoning. He always had the spirit of reconciliation toward his adversaries and longed for public debate and scriptural basis for discussion on all these issues. Unable to prove him wrong, they always resorted to falsehood in order to gain support of civil authorities to silence him.

At the Council of Protestant States in 1556 Schwenckfeld was denounced in the most un-Christian language of the period and the civil authorities were instructed to treat him as a heretic. However, "he always had ... many powerful friends and a large number of brave devoted followers who were glad to risk goods, home and life for the sake of what was to them the living Word of God."[66] In all this controversy he

---

[63] Paul Maier, *Caspar Schwenckfeld ...*, is an excellent presentation of Schwenckfeld's Christology.

[64] Jones, *op. cit.*, p. 69.

[65] S. Schultz, *Caspar Schwenckfeld ...*, p. 257.

[66] Jones, *op. cit.*, p. 69.

took time for study, Bible reading, prayer and writing of pastoral letters to his friends. He was friend to all classes and to all conditions of men. He sought spiritual unity based on love wherever he went and in whatever he did.

From 1554 to 1559 his name was dragged in the mud of hatred due to misrepresentation and evil rumor. He had to move from one hide-out to another. In spite of all hardship he continued steadfast in his convictions and loyal to his cause.

5. Last Days

Near the end of his life Schwenckfeld wrote,[67]

> The aim and purpose of our ministry is to praise Christ, the ruling king of grace, to bear witness of him and his benefits by scriptural testimony and through him to point to God in all matters pertaining to religion. We remain humble and do not presume anything other than that we bear witness of Christ, invite everyone to him, preach Christ and his boundless mercies and endeavor to make Christ really known.

In spite of this high aim and sincere practice of his religion, Schwenckfeld was heavily persecuted. It seams, however, that his only crime was that he believed Christian unity is to be found in the Spirit of God, not in compromise, forced creeds or ceremonies, and that he believed more in the authority of Christ than in the authority of the Roman Catholic or even the Reformation churches. On his deathbed he forgave all who had opposed him and prayed for their well being.

Broken in health, burdened with age and haunted by the fear of martyrdom, Schwenckfeld died in Ulm, December 10, 1561. According to one tradition he was probably buried under the Streicher house which today is the center of an intersection of two streets in Ulm. Another tradition claims he was interred in the crypt of the chapel in the castle of Oepfingen, about sixteen miles beyond the limits of Ulm.

The Schwenckfelder Movement perished as such in Southern Germany during the Thirty Years War, 1618—1648. His ideas, however, were implanted throughout Europe and finally came to America in several waves between 1732 and 1737, with the largest group of immigrants arriving in Philadelphia September 22, 1734. On the 24th, they held

---

[67] S. Schultz, *Course of Study . . .*, p. 36.

a Day of Thanksgiving for their safe journey. This day has been observed each year ever since as a Day of Remembrance.

> The memory of Caspar Schwenckfeld will live on in the Christian Church as that of a true pupil and teacher in the school of Christ. Others have surpassed him as thinkers and theologians, and not a few as leaders and organizers of Christian group life, but not many in saintliness of character, in love for Jesus Christ, and in zeal for the cause of the Gospel. [68]

---

[68] Joachim Wach, "Caspar Schwenckfeld, a Pupil and a Teacher in the School of Christ," *The Journal of Religion.* Vol. XXVI, Number 1, (Chicago: The University of Chicago Press, January, 1946), p. 169.

CHAPTER III

INFLUENCES UPON SCHWENCKFELD

1. Roman Catholicism

> After so many centuries of error we cannot expect to
> correct everything in a few short years.
>
> CASPAR SCHWENCKFELD

Although Caspar Schwenckfeld was born and reared in a pious Roman Catholic family of importance in his homeland, the influence of the Roman Catholic Church upon him was great only in a negative way. Because of the conditions in the church during his boyhood and the rising tide of bitterness among the people of Silesia due to the oppressive methods of the clergy, it is safe to say the young Schwenckfeld received more "Christian" influence from his pious parents than he ever received from his church.

Precarious social conditions, impossible financial problems, double standards for clergy and laity, schisms among the clergy, immorality practiced in the very name of the church, the evils of indulgence and the emphasis upon external means of getting to heaven while being under the coercive thumbs of ignorant, superstitious and unlearned priests, all due largely to the Roman Catholic Church of his day, certainly must have had a tremendous influence on the young, fertile mind and loving heart of Caspar Schwenckfeld—an influence that literally drove him to seek freedom and unity among all who called upon Christ as Savior and Lord.

2. Luther and the Lutherans

When Schwenckfeld read Luther's *Call to the German Nobility* in 1518, he was deeply moved by the spiritual nature of the kind of reform

28

being sought by the leader of the Reformation. He sought to follow Luther's summons with heart and soul. He read everything Luther wrote and eagerly sought his friendship throughout his life. "From the beginning of the Reformation Schwenckfeld accepted Luther as a messenger from God, by whose trumpet call against the false worship of God by anti-Christ he was roused in 1518."[69] For eight years after his awakening, Schwenckfeld considered himself a coworker in the Lutheran Reformation, seeking to make it more than just an external cleansing of the church. He had won the warm friendship of Luther during these years and Luther considered him a good preacher.[70]

In 1528, he was still convinced that Lutheranism would win against the Papacy, even though he could not, by that date, agree with the direction of Lutheranism in all details. As late as 1546, even though he had been cruelly rebuffed by Luther and the "orthodox" Lutherans, he continued to pray for the cause of Protestantism and was still convinced, in spite of the coercive methods, that there was more hope for religious freedom in the future under Protestant than under Roman Catholic dominion. He urged his followers to pray always for the success of the Protestant cause, even to his dying days.[71] When Martin Luther died in 1546, Caspar was deeply shaken by the loss.

The times required a personality like Luther's, rather than that of Schwenckfeld, to get the Reformation off the ground and this writer is convinced Schwenckfeld understood that. Nevertheless, he knew that Lutheranism was heading back into a dry orthodoxy and was not bringing to pass what Luther himself had intended in the early years of his reformatory efforts. Up to 1525, Schwenckfeld had traveled the road of religious reform with Luther. But in Luther's dealings with the Peasant's Revolt, in his ever increasing dogmatic spirit, and his emphasis upon institutional Christianity and its stress on externals and literalism, Schwenckfeld had to part company externally with Luther. He felt Luther was compromising too much of the Protestant cause for the sake of political strength and safety or for the sake of external church unity. For Schwenckfeld, there could be no compromise between the spiritual and the carnal.

---

[69] S. Schultz, *Caspar Schwenckfeld* . . . , p. 18.
[70] *CS.*, IX, 82.
[71] *Ibid.*, IX, preface xii.

He could not go along with the Lutherans and other Protestant groups who were seeking Christian unity through compulsory adherence to man-made creeds and organizations or strained theological theories for the sake of concord. Rather, the unity of the Church of Jesus Christ, accord-ing to Schwenckfeld, must be built on, (1) the knowledge of Christ, (2) the spiritual interpretation of Scripture, (3) liberty of spirit, (4) faith in God, i. e., complete surrender to God's will, and (5) a free conscience. Of these fundamentals Schwenckfeld could accept no compromise.

In spite of their differences, Luther held a compelling influence upon Schwenckfeld all his life and even when they disagreed, the disagreement helped Schwenckfeld search deeper into the validity of his own thinking by driving him to a more thorough study of the Scriptures and reliance upon prayer and Divine guidance.

Luther's influence upon Schwenckfeld was great. However, Schwenck-feld's criticism of Lutheranism after 1525 was very strong.[72] As early as 1528 Schwenckfeld said that Luther's work had run its course and his doctrines were now tending to destroy rather than build up the external church. Schwenckfeld said:

1) Luther's doctrine of the Lord's Supper was becoming a new indul-gence.

2) Lutheranism was a literal, carnal kingdom, a relapse into Catholi-cism because it united church and state.

3) The dissensions among Protestants would not have come had Luther continued to maintain the difference between the spiritual and the literal or external as he did early in his career, before 1525.

4) When Luther changed direction, he was powerful enough to drag nearly everyone interested in reforming the church down with him.[73]

3. Erasmus and Humanism

Humanism was a valuable preparation for the Reformation Era and formed a very vital part of the Era itself. Religious humanism, the type characterized by Erasmus of Rotterdam, helped the Reformation in the

---

[72] S. Schultz, loc. cit., p. 367.
[73] CS. II, 330, 642, 682; III, 10; IX, 42, 43, 46, 89—90, 91, 134, 719; X, 836; XI, 87, 220, 958; XII, 248—263; 808—819; XIII, 775, 897; XIV, 885, 977, 1014; XVI Doc. MXXXV.

following ways: (1) It helped to expose the vice and corruption taking place under the guise of religion. (2) It condemned the uselessness of externals in giving spiritual depth to life. (3) It stressed the inwardness of true religion by its emphasis upon the necessity to "know oneself." (4) It put great emphasis upon education and saw that a gradual change is more lasting and more effective than a rapid, spectacular reform. (5) It pointed to the great potential that lies, usually untapped, in man.

However, humanism had its weaknesses too. (1) It failed to grasp the truth that it is not education alone, but a vital religious faith wedded to education that can nourish the human soul. (2) It failed to see that even man's reason has been affected by sin and needs redemption. (3) It also failed to see that it is not man's effort by himself that works for the highest good, but that it is only by God's grace that man has any right to work or any strength to accomplish what is lasting. (4) It always stops short of any real satisfaction for the deepest spiritual needs of man because: (5) It usually fails to see man as a sinner in need of repentance and redemption.

Desiderius Erasmus of Rotterdam gave the necessary controls to the Reformation, without which it might have ended in total fanaticism and/or total destruction of the Christian church. Because of his uncompromising, mature view of the dignity of man, his striving for unity of spirit among all Christians, his emphasis on the inwardness of true religion as well as the necessity of religion to be expressed in outward conduct, and the centrality of Christ in his thinking, we see Erasmus as a Christian Humanist whose contributions to Christian thought gave much to all sides of the Reformation, but especially to the central stream of "experiential Christianity" of which Caspar Schwenckfeld is one of the noblest representatives in the sixteenth century.

While being the "prince of the Renaissance men" [74] and the great popularizer of the classics, he was not content to deal only in the past. While recognizing the great dignity of man and the values to be found in Humanism, he remained Christocentric. While deeply concerned with the events of his day, he preferred to remain a spectator in the hope of keeping the unity of Christendom in the future.

---

[74] Matthew Spinka, *Advocates of Reform,* (Philadelphia: The Westminster Press, 1953), p. 281.

Erasmus was attempting the complete reorganization of his world partly through comparison with the ideas of the maturer minds of the past, and partly through the inspired common sense of his own mind, having before him the ideals of the Gospel. This immense vision had grown upon him slowly, and was coming to fruition in the years 1514—18 at Bäle. Those years placed him in his central and supreme position at the very heart of the Renaissance. [75]

Thus, as a "Renaissance Man" he was a man of his age but, as an independent Christian thinker and contributor to an age just beginning—"Erasmus laid the egg that was later hatched by Luther." He set the stage and pointed in the direction of sincere historical criticism of the Bible in an attempt to restore the Christian church to simplicity, inwardness and practical goodness. He seems to have put more significance in the religion of Jesus than in a "proper theology" about Jesus.

Foreign to his thinking was the type of humanism which imagines man as supreme Lord of the universe, needing no God to inspire and no Christ to redeem him. He valued man and all his works and contributed much to the rebirth of confidence in the innate powers of the human mind, but he was always a Christian humanist. Christ was central. He sought to use the wisdom of the ancients in order to interpret Christianity for the betterment of man. This was his purpose and life goal. [76]

He did not create a denomination and his writings are not read today by anyone except the research scholar. But, it seems quite possible that the ecumenical movement today is close to his ideal of harmony in diversity. In his own lifetime he saw only failure and the threat of great war between the religious groups ahead.

Like Erasmus, Schwenckfeld worked diligently for a transformation of individual life so that a truly "religious" reformation of the Church would result. He was convinced that Jesus delivered religion from outward ceremonial form and "ivory tower" correctness and made it individual and inward. He put the accent upon simplicity as the best outward adornment for the Spirit. [77] He said that the end of grace is to make a man essentially better and to make that betterment tell upon his neighbor's welfare. [78] This kind of religion is not anything that is studied in books or in seminaries but is the direct working of the Holy Spirit in

---

[75] Margaret Mann Phillips, *Erasmus and the Northern Renaissance,* (New York: The Macmillan Company, 1950), p. 71.

[76] *Ibid.*, pp. 44, 62, 77, 78, 80.

[77] CS., I xxxii.   [78] *Ibid.*, xxxvi.

the hearts and minds of believers and this inner working shows increasingly in outward behavior.

Again like Erasmus, Schwenckfeld saw that Jesus dethroned the theologians of his time and preached not as the learned but as one who was inspired. He said "the official Christian and the nominal religionist alike are to be judged wholly by their conduct."[79]

Schwenckfeld was well educated and well read in the literature of the scholastics, humanists, Church Fathers, the sermons of Johannes Tauler, the publications of Luther, Erasmus, Hutten and others soon after they appeared from the press.[80] He read all literature critically, diligently and minutely, with discrimination, for he believed that all these were subject to error. But like Erasmus he believed that no amount of critical study could cause a true Christian to err. He determined to investigate all matters pertaining to faith, for "our faith is not darkness, but a light and an assurance of the things which we believe and hope."[81]

Among his studies were Erasmus' *Annotations of the New Testament* which he cherished very highly. Dr. Selina Schultz claims, however, that his use of these studies merely entrenched Schwenckfeld still more deeply in the ideas and views which he had already attained. In 1526—1527 Schwenckfeld often gave credit to Erasmus for his best study of the Scriptures. From Erasmus' grammatical constructions of the New Testament Schwenckfeld arrived at his views on the Lord's Supper and justification in particular.[82]

Like Erasmus, whom Schwenckfeld never met personally as far as present records indicate, Schwenckfeld was more interested in religious life than he was in "formal theology." Yet in spite of his much study and great learning, unlike Erasmus, Schwenckfeld remained close to the people. Theology is of secondary import—it is necessary only to help interpret religion to the outer man. Like Erasmus, he always distinguished between the inner and outer in all things and gave priority to the inner. In all he said, did and wrote, Schwenckfeld, like Erasmus, remained Christocentric and endeavored to work for unity of Spirit among all Christians. The "knowledge of Christ," similar to Erasmus' "philosophy of Christ," Schwenckfeld said is the one thing needful. "Nil Triste, Christo Recepto" (Having Christ I am not sad) was his motto for life.

---

[79] *Ibid.,* I, xxxvii.
[81] *Ibid.,* p. 28.

[80] S. Schultz, *op. cit.,* p. 9.
[82] *Ibid.,* pp. 324, 346, 378.

To Erasmus must go the credit for much of Schwenckfeld's Bible interpretations. With the new philology of Erasmus, Schwenckfeld plunged into fresh waters of the original texts. It has been said that the Latin of Schwenckfeld's writings is assuredly equal if not superior to any example of the literature of correspondence in this period. "Neither the Ciceronians nor the Erasmians captured him; there is no imitative quality in it, it is as fresh and original as any bit of dead language can be." [83]

Further evidence of the influence of Erasmus upon Schwenckfeld is seen in the fact of Schwenckfeld's urging Crautwald to use the new techniques of Erasmus for Biblical study. [84] His translation of the Bible anticipates the Revised Standard Version very closely. [85] Schwenckfeld quotes much from the *Adgia* of Erasmus and reveals a marked fondness for proverbs similar to that of Erasmus. [86] In Schwenckfeld's *Deutsch Passional* which was his most popular book of prayers we find many similarities and borrowings from Erasmus' *Precationes aliquot novae*. [87]

To be sure, Schwenckfeld did break with the Roman Church whereas Erasmus did not, but he tended to stand aloof from the popular stream of the Reformation like Erasmus because it had become not only a religious movement but also a political movement in which he felt the church and state were no longer separate. Any alliance between church and state was foreign to his conception of Christianity. The individual conscience is to be free. He loved freedom perhaps even more than Erasmus because, at least formally, Erasmus remained within the Church of Rome. Schwenckfeld believed the individual conscience cannot be dictated to by prince or priest. Thus he decided not to meddle with the shifting policies which rolled their troubled waves about him. He felt the Reformation leaders were rapidly losing their religious spontaneity and he constantly warned against new forms of papacy. [88] Schwenckfeld tended to separate himself from a rigid Augustinianism in regard to free will. In this he was close to Erasmus, [89] but he was always firm in opposing the semi-palaganism of Erasmus—he early took a scriptural position against atheistic and fatalistic tendencies of many other humanists as well. [90]

---

[83] *CS.*, I, 16.
[84] *Ibid.*, II, 179.
[85] S. Schultz, *op. cit.*, p. 22.
[86] *CS.*, I, 17.
[87] *Ibid.*, VI, 653.
[88] *Ibid.*, IV, preface.
[89] *Ibid.*, II, 684.
[90] *Ibid.*, IV, 88.

Although the popular thrust of the Reformation went against Erasmus and Schwenckfeld, we must remember that mere popularity is not the true measure of greatness. It is most likely true that the robust sixteenth century needed the temperament of a Luther, a Calvin and a Loyola and we are certainly grateful to these and others like them for their great contribution to the life of the church, but we must never forget that the piety and confidence in the potentialities of man, the inwardness, simplicity and noncompromising attitude of an Erasmus and a Schwenckfeld were needed to carry on what is too deep for words in the life of the church.

Huizinga[91] says that among the vehemently passionate, drastically energetic and violent natures of the great ones of his day, Erasmus stands as the man of too few prejudices with a little too much delicacy of taste. Erasmus is the man who is too sensible and moderate for the heroic. He seems at times to be a man not strong enough for his age and yet strong enough to be the teacher of every age—a precursor of the modern spirit. He was an introducer and initiator of a new age. Others after him such as Schwenckfeld carried his work further toward more definite ends. "Eventually neither camp finally rejected Erasmus. Rome did not brand him an arch-heretic, but only warned the faithful to read him with caution. Protestant history has been studious to reckon him as one of the Reformers."[92]

We think of Erasmus mainly as the one who wrote for a wide public and helped extend a knowledge of classical culture throughout Europe and thus to all the world of today. The one who is characterized by the spirit of gentleness, kindliness, moderation and tolerance, whose biblical studies opened the way to exegetical research which is still going on today. The one who, although not a rationalist himself, held reason in high regard and was the apostle of common sense and a great liberator of the mind and heart. Finally, we think of Erasmus as the one who led the way to the ecumenical spirit of unity in diversity, pacifism and international understanding which is so much needed today.

It is certain that his emphases helped to influence the thinking of Caspar Schwenckfeld von Ossig.

---

[91] Johan Huizinga, *Erasmus and the Age of Reformation,* (New York: Harper Torchbook, 1957), p. 188.

[92] *Ibid.,* p. 192.

4. Tauler and Mysticism

It was his avoidance of a crude and magical reliance on faith which drove Schwenckfeld to a deeper study of religion. He felt a necessity to discover some way by which man himself could be actually renewed, transformed, recreated, and made righteous—rather than merely counted or reckoned righteous by some magical transaction—that made him an independent reformer and set him on his solitary way.[93]

Schwenckfeld was not satisfied with any of the prevailing ways of salvation in his day, namely: (1) The Roman Catholic way which said salvation is by Grace mediated through the sacramental channels of the mysterious and divinely founded church and by man's performance of the works required by the church. (2) The mystical way of salvation through a pantheistic conception of the world in which only a union and oneness of life with the Ground-Reality gives salvation. (3) The Lutheran interpretation of the biblical phrase "Salvation is by faith" seems dynamic but Luther and the Lutherans never quite escaped from scholastic interpretations of this and it never really affected the moral or practical life of the people. To Schwenckfeld, imputed righteousness was not what Jesus was speaking of in the Sermon on the Mount and it was not the kind of salvation spoken of in the Johannine and Pauline writings. (4) The humanistic-spiritual way of salvation characterized by Denck and Bünderlin who were the forerunners of the ethical societies of today. Salvation for these people is simply a moral process. Those who respond to God in Christ and cooperate ethically with him become morally transformed and they prefer goodness to sin, love to hate, and light to darkness.

Schwenckfeld could see value in each of these ways of salvation except in the Roman Catholic, but he could not choose one and say that is what Christian salvation is. He loved the mystical approach but was too much concerned with the historical Christ to be called a typical mystic. He liked Luther's original intent but felt Lutheranism was overly scholastic and too dependent upon externals with little or no emphasis upon discipline in the Christian life. He believed man was sinful and every aspect of humanity was affected by the Fall and therefore man was

---

[93] Jones, *op. cit.*, p. 75.

helpless without the Spirit to live morally as the humanist-spirituals seemed to think he could.

"Justification is not only forgiveness of sins, but it is more, it is the actual healing and renewing of the inward man," according to Schwenckfeld.[94] It involves a real and radical change in man's nature—man receives from beyond himself a passion for goodness and a power to enable him to do the Will of God. This passion and power is given to man by the direct inflowing of divine Life-Streams from Christ who is the head of the spiritual order of humanity.[95]

The true Church is the complete spiritual community of which Christ is the head. The true mark of membership in this community is the actual possession of the mind of Christ, faith, patience, integrity, peace, unity of spirit, the power of God, joy in the Holy Ghost, and the abounding gifts and fruits of the Spirit. Schwenckfeld's first concern was the building of the invisible community of God throughout the whole world. He believed that the visible church had lost its original power and authority because of its neglect of inward religion and he hoped and believed that God would eventually restore his Church to its original form and purpose. He firmly held that "the only way to form an apostolic and efficacious visible Church is not through sudden miracles and cataclysmic "restorations" and "commissions," but by the slow contagion and conquering power of this inward kingdom, of this invisible Church, as it becomes the spirit and life of the outward and visible church."[96]

To arrive at such views, Schwenckfeld was influenced by the great mystics. "The oldest spring of German mystical literature from which Schwenckfeld drank was Tauler."[97] Dr. Seyppel points out that Sebastian Franck, a contemporary of Schwenckfeld and an acquaintance, and Jacob Boehme, a successor to many Schwenckfeldian ideas, as well as Schwenckfeld himself were all much influenced by the mystical writings of Tauler. But each had to say both yes and no to each other on various points. Dr. Schultz insists that Schwenckfeld always discounted humanistic, spiritualistic and speculative mystical works of the medieval mystics[98] and

---

[94] *Ibid.*, p. 77.

[95] This is similar to the doctrine of deification in Irenaeus.

[96] Jones, *op. cit.*, p. 86.

[97] Seyppel, *op. cit.*, chap. iv, p. 80 ff.

[98] *CS.*, IV, 519; VI, 70—78, 541; VII, 152; VIII, Doc. CCCXCII; VIII, 210, 212, 469; IX; 791; CS. Biography, p. 375.

combatted by argument with many of his contemporaries such as Sebastian Franck, Christian Entfelder, Hans Denck, Hans Bünderlin, Theophrastus Paracelsus, *et al.* In every discussion on these "mystical" matters Schwenckfeld emerged as an independent thinker. He placed no value on such things commonly held as mystical, as religious ecstasy, enthusiasm and he said all pantheistic trends are at variance with scripture.

Schwenckfeld was fundamentally Bible oriented in his thinking and in his religious life. His Christ-mysticism rested upon his own spiritual experiences as interpreted by his study of the Bible. He regarded Johannes Tauler as a great Christian mystic but he also felt Tauler was not Christocentric enough and should be read with discretion. Although Schwenckfeld read most mystical writings of his day, he instructed others to hold to the brighter light, *i. e.,* to the Scriptures wherein Christ is mentioned more frequently.[99]

Schwenckfeld was influenced by the depth of mysticism in stressing the inward realities but his own form of mysticism was profoundly based upon his own spiritual experience and the real presence of Christ in his life.[100]

5. Religious existence

"The causes that produced a Schwenckfeld in Germany, a Pascal in France, a Kierkegaard in Denmark were ... materially different, but like in form, and therefore their effects were like."[101] Such persons become disturbers of the status quo, a nuisance to the institutional church, rebels against false security at a time when man, either knowingly or unknowingly, stands before the abyss of nothingness.

In Schwenckfeld, as in the others mentioned above, we find a genuine Christian life blended with a Christ-mysticism which challenges life as it is popularly conceived. According to Dr. Seyppel, Schwenckfeld and

---

[99] S. Schultz, *op. cit.,* p. 376.

[100] Dr. Seyppel clearly shows the influence of Tauler upon Schwenckfeld in Chapter 4 and points out the difference in tone between the two. On page 98 he says: "he feels himself close to Tauler and Franck, otherwise he would not have cared to discuss them at all ... he was alone in his Christological spiritualism. Tauler and Franck are closer to each other than to Schwenckfeld, and Schwenckfeld remains the lonely apostle of a Christian life that demanded everything or nothing ... no middle path here."

[101] Seyppel, *op. cit.,* chap. 5, p. 114.

Pascal and Kierkegaard belong together because of their spiritual religion, their affiliation with mysticism, their rejection of the rationalistic systems, their opposition to organized and superficial church-and-state-Christianity. "They cross church lines and stand in the middle road, the road of the individualist." [102] Nevertheless, we must remind ourselves that Schwenckfeld was always the layman, pastor-apostle type and not the ivory tower thinker.

Søren Kierkegaard is claimed by a variety of existentialist philosophers such as Heidegger, Jaspers, Sarte, Camus, Berdyaev and other Greek-Orthodox thinkers, Marcel, Buber, Barth, Protestant Neo-Orthodoxy and others. He is hailed by all as the father of modern existentialism. He had only one vital concern in life—a true religion.

Although differing in temperament both from Pascal and Schwenckfeld, we must note a similarity in intent and purpose and therefore place them all in the same "stream of the Holy Spirit" which continues to nourish the Christian Church through the centuries. Dr. Joachim Wach [103] drew many similarities between Schwenckfeld and Kierkegaard. "Both Schwenckfeld and Kierkegaard aimed at life, at the individual, at the person's fate Here and There." [104] Schwenckfeld often repeated "each man must himself account to God" [105] and thus refused to form a sect or join a church. Both Schwenckfeld and Kierkegaard had deep personal religious experiences early in their careers—Schwenckfeld at age twenty eight and Kierkegaard at age twenty five. Both rejected the external, literal, systems of Christianity. Dr. Seyppel says that both lived lonely, persecuted lives and "soon half or wholly forgotten, their respective ideas had a different fate: While Schwenckfeld's flowered into Pietism without being recognized as his, Kierkegaard's flowered in Existentialism where they cannot be recognized any more as his." [106] Schwenckfeld prepared the way for the kind of Pietism in which Kierkegaard grew up into maturity. He was deeply influenced by his pious father to put all the emphasis on the personal life and commitment of the Christian individual to Christ in order to attain righteous living. "Schwenckfeld was 'the first knight' of existence-bound Pietism, and Kierkegaard became the theoretician of the 'knight of faith' in pietistic armor." [107]

---

102 *Ibid.*, p. 118.
104 Seyppel, *op. cit.*, p. 125.
106 Seyppel, *op. cit.*, p. 126.

103 Wach, *op. cit.*, p. 103.
105 *CS.*, V, 101.
107 *Ibid.*, p. 129.

Existence for Schwenckfeld was an abyss from which Christ rescues the repentant sinner, for Kierkegaard it was a depth out of which man had to climb himself by virtue of his existential freedom. Both these men viewed life as misery, but Schwenckfeld found in Christ the only "person" whom we could grasp to take us out of misery because he had become man, although not a creature. "Nil Triste Christo Recepto" expresses Schwenckfeld's grasp upon Christ. To both these men, outward Christianity, material sacramentarianism, church collectivity, etc., are rejected as "means of grace." These things represent a petrified Christendom when the depth of existence is not held most important. There is or can be no real Christianity when one's religion is based solely upon outward forms and intellectual acceptance of what the churches dictate.

Both Kierkegaard and Schwenckfeld said that there can be no lukewarm Christian or Christianity. Either you are a Christian, a Christ follower possessed by His Spirit, or you are not. Either you live by faith or you don't. Faith is an enduring seizure or passion for Christ. It is being deeply stirred, deeply affected or struck by the reality of Christ in your life. It is a two way action, God's possession of us and our grasping God in Christ. It is both action and surrender at the same time. In Christian faith, a person is alone before his God and there can be no retreat once self is committed to Him. This self-surrender to Christ, faith, is not-communicable by any material means. One cannot have faith for someone else. It is deeply personal and individual. But it shows in one's life and behavior when it is present. Men of faith can have worldwide community.

Dr. Seyppel says Schwenckfeld lived Christian existence according to the pattern set by Christ and which Kierkegaard attempted to re-establish theoretically.[108]

Undoubtedly there were other influences upon Schwenckfeld, but the ones mentioned in this chapter seem to be the dominant ones having influence upon his ecumenical ideal.

---

[108] *Ibid.*, p. 145.

CHAPTER IV

THE ECUMENICAL IDEAL

1. The Call to Unity.

"What must I do to be saved?" is no longer a religious question only in our kind of world. It has become a question of human survival: The answer one gives to this question, which was also the dominant question of the sixteenth century as well as the first century and of every century before and after that time, has much to do with the question of Christian unity. The world of the sixteenth century, as we have seen, was very much like our own. It was a world of new ideas, new methods, new discoveries, new dangers, new opportunities for good and for evil. Although we today have more of everything and our explorations and inventions reduce the size of our universe even smaller than in those days, and although we have the opportunity for greater good and greater evil, we still face the same ultimate fears and anxieties and we still have to answer the same question: "What must I do to be saved?"

It appears that the mission or task of the Church of Jesus Christ has not been altered since the time of the first century. To be sure, this was God's purpose in creating the world. That purpose is our call to Christian unity. It is true that the Church of Jesus Christ is one in reality because Christ is its unity, or rather, it is his Body, but it is also true that the church as we know it is not one in actuality. Our Lord's Prayer in John 17 has not yet been realized in the experience of men. Nevertheless, the New Testament message and the thrust of history point in the direction of such unity. The teaching of the Bible concerning the essential oneness of the Church is perfectly clear.[109] However, the Bible fails to give us any detailed plan for the form or structure of the United Church

---

[109] Among many other references we note Ephesians 1 : 10, 4 : 3.

and therefore the visible church has become divided due to our varied interpretations of Christ's will for his Church. Nevertheless, "the Church must be one if it is to be God's instrument for unifying the entire world in Christ."[110]

It is evident that the present divisions in the Body of Christ are contrary to God's will. Jesus declared his will that the Church should be one, "there shall be one flock, one shepherd" (John 10:16). St. Paul taught repeatedly that the Body of Christ cannot be divided and he even used the symbol of the Eucharist to illustrate this unity: "Because there is one loaf, we who are many are one body, for we all partake of the same loaf," (I Corinthians 10:16). However, Paul also taught that within this one Body of Christ there can be "varieties of gifts," "variaties of service," and "varieties of working," (I Corinthians 12:4ff). The great creeds of the Christian Church testify to the belief in the unity of the Church. The ecumenical movement of today assumes the churches cannot long exist without experiential unity.

In spite of the general belief in the unity of the Church, we still are hindered by denominations numbering nearly three hundred today. About ten of these comprise ninety five percent of all professing Christians in the world. Many of these groups are in keen competition with all the rest. Some are concerned only with their own interests. Only a few are seriously working at solving the problem of a divided appearance in a divided world that is desperately in search of the answer to its question: "What must we do to be saved?"

The search for church unity is a reopening of the discussions which motivated and fired the Reformation Era and caused the many divisions in the first place. "The reunion of the churches will not emerge merely from summit conferences of ecumenical experts, indispensable though they are. It will come when the unity is seen first of all as a call to mission. He who issues this call is still one God. His call is one call, and the gospel of reconciliation between man and God and man and man is still one gospel."[111]

---

[110] Morgren, *International Journal of Religious Education*, November, 1961, p. 5.
[111] Wedel, *Ibid.*, p. 8.

2. A Brief History of the Ecumenical Movement.

Bridge of Unity
The eye can see a thousand things
A sunset cloud, a cardinal's wings.
Would that the inner eye could find
The bridge uniting all mankind.[112]

Christianity, in its modern dress confronts the world both as a message and as a movement. The message is "God so loved . . . that He gave . . . that whoever believes . . . may have life." The message is Christ ! ! The movement, if it is to be true to its founder, must be centered in the message.

The movement begun by Jesus presented the world of the first century with a new hope, but at the expense of the *status quo* and the possessors of status. Herod Antipas feared that John the Baptist had returned and he was filled with fear. Jesus' enemies tried to represent him and his movement in such a way that Pontius Pilate, fearing for his position, consented to Jesus' death in order to stop a possible revolution. But he could not stop the kind of revolution Jesus brought for it was within the hearts and minds of men.

Jesus had taken steps to give some form to his movement by choosing and training certain men to be his disciples, the inner circle of three, the twelve, the seventy. He trained these people, "inspired" them, and sent them out to proclaim the message and develop the movement. After his resurrection and ascension, and on the Day of Pentecost, the Christian movement as a world wide expansion of a Church already in existence began with renewed vigor. Jesus himself had entered his Church and gave it power to become the redeeming fellowship for all mankind.

This was in the early days of the ecumenical movement. Of course, the modern ecumenical movement usually takes its starting date as the Edinburgh Conference in 1910. However, ". . . the ecumenical movement is a living movement which has no date, no emergence and no end. It cannot be judged by the conferences and assemblies that the World Council of Churches arranges because the ecumenical movement is bigger than its organizational outcroppings."[113]

---

[112] *The Christian Century*, May 26, 1954, p. 634. Lucia Trent (used by permission).
[113] Cecil Northcott, "Prospectus for the Church," *The Christian Century*, February 15, 1961.

Nevertheless, in our day, the ecumenical movement is symbolized and organized in the form known as the World Council of Churches. The conciliar movements on local, state, national and world levels are here considered integral parts of the entire ecumenical movement. The word we use today to describe Christian unity is oikoumene-ecumenical, which means "the whole inhabited earth." At first this word was used to refer only to geography, that is, "the whole world is the field of the church's activity." Gradually the word came to have a deeper meaning in which the total Household of Faith or the Church Universal or the Holy Catholic Church was meant. Today we use the word ecumenical to express Christian unity, rising above national boundaries, above church divisions and differences, above race and above specific creeds. "We are all responsible for the fate of mankind."[114]

The World Council of Churches is a fellowship of Christians seeking unity, understanding, service, prayer and growth in the knowledge of Christ for the purpose of reconciliation.[115] It is not its purpose to negotiate church unions for only churches themselves can do that.[116] Membership in the World Council of Churches is open to any communion or denomination who can subscribe to the following statement: "The World Council of Churches is a fellowship of churches which confess the Lord Jesus Christ as God and Savior according to the Scriptures and therefore seek to fulfill together their common calling to the glory of the one God, Father, Son and Holy Spirit."[117]

In 1961 the World Council of Churches contained one hundred and ninety seven denominations from sixty nations representing around two hundred and twenty five million persons. It is the result of more than fifty years of inter-denominational, international and interracial cooperation. It has reached such proportions that in one way or another every Christian must come to terms with this movement. Christians cannot honestly ignore or neglect the New Testament mandate to seek for unity

---

[114] Eivind Berggrav, "World Tensions and Unity in Christ," *The Christian Century,* September 15, 1954.

[115] Kathleen Bliss, "What Is the World Council?," *The Christian Century,* September 15, 1954.

[116] Angus Dun, "The World Council Still Seeks Unity," (Statement of Central Committee, World Council of Churches, Toronto, 1950), *The Christian Century,* August 11, 1954.

[117] Last revised at New Delhi, 1961.

44

and continue to call themselves Christian. The ecumenical movement, as embodied in the World Council of Churches addresses itself primarily to the problem of division and disunity that exists today within Christendom.

The greatest single motivation in the history of this movement has been the growing realization and emphasis upon the total mission of the church in the world. In 1910 at Edinburgh a conference was called to plan over-all missionary strategy and to explore ways for separate Christian bodies to work together in unity of purpose. By 1921 the International Missionary Council was formed out of twenty-eight cooperating missionary agencies of the world.

The history of the World Council of Churches reveals that the purpose is not merely to present a united front, but to seek and promote a growing power against the forces of secularism and immorality and sin in the world.

The Edinburgh Conference stimulated the search for greater Christian unity in other areas of the churches. The Life and Work Movement based upon the belief that Christians can realize their oneness when engaged in common task on the practical levels of the day by day work-a-day world. This movement was organized in 1937 at Oxford.

Edinburgh also gave the "go" sign to others who caught the vision of Christian unity along doctrinal lines. A World Conference of Faith and Order was called in 1927 at Lausanne, Switzerland.

All three movements succeeded well and followed separate paths for a while but eventually their lives touched and the leaders became aware that theology, ethics and missions belong together. In 1938, Life and Work and Faith and Order formed the first World Council of Churches. The first assembly of this new body was not held until 1948 because of the second World War. It was held in Amsterdam. The World Council of Churches met in General Assembly again in 1954 at Evanston, Illinois and in New Delhi, India in 1961. At New Delhi the International Missionary Council joined forces in organizational structure in an effort to halt some overlapping of activity.

This organization, with headquarters in Geneva Switzerland, is the strongest voice the Church has today in the world to witness to our oneness in Christ. It is attempting to rediscover the Church by acknowledging its central unity in Jesus Christ.

The history of the ecumenical movement to date has shown that it is not primarily an organization, not a super-church, not unity on the basis of the least common denominator, but it is seriously seeking the fulfilment of the unity God has given by answering the Call of Christ.[118]

Schematic History of the World Council of Churches

"Ecumenical"—The world-wide scope of the Church's fellowship and the world-wide range of its task. The whole Church in the whole inhabited world.

The original source of the movement is the Christian Faith itself. It is that spiritual power which draws men together in Christ and then sends them out in his name to claim the whole οικουμενη for him.

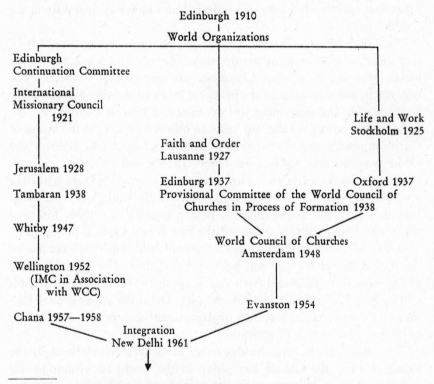

Edinburgh 1910
|
World Organizations

Edinburgh
Continuation Committee
|
International
Missionary Council
    1921
                                        Life and Work
                                        Stockholm 1925

                    Faith and Order
                    Lausanne 1927

Jerusalem 1928
    | Edinburg 1937   Oxford 1937
Tambaran 1938   Provisional Committee of the World Council of
                        Churches in Process of Formation 1938

Whitby 1947
                            World Council of Churches
                                Amsterdam 1948

Wellington 1952
    (IMC in Association
    with WCC)
                            Evanston 1954

Chana 1957—1958
                    Integration
                New Delhi 1961

---

[118] Norman Goodall, *The Exumenical Movement: What It Is and What It Does*, (New York: Oxford University Press, 1961).

46

3. Ecumenical Concerns

> "The ecumenical movement is far from being fully ecumenical."
>
> VISSER 'T HOOFT [119]

The main concern of the ecumenical movement today is this: How can our present unity grow toward the unity which is biblically normal. [120] Unity cannot be static. It must grow when Christians put themselves at God's disposal. It must die when God is forgotten and the Spirit is not given freedom to direct. "The ecumenical task is to go forward together in making a common response to the one calling." [121] Only those people who are selfcentered and seek their own glory rather than the glory of God are people who are indifferent to the ecumenical nature of the church. The very roots of the ecumenical movement lie deep in the very purpose of God in sending his Son to this earth. "As thou didst send me into the world, so I have sent them into the world" (John 17:18, also see 12:47, 3:16, I John 4:14). [122]

We must constantly remind ourselves "however deep and broad our agreement may be, if it is not rooted in and controlled by the faith once delivered to the saints, it is not the unity for which our Lord prayed." [123]

The express purpose of Christian unity is to convince the world that Jesus is truly sent by God and that God loves and seeks his scattered children everywhere. This cannot happen so long as the visible churches remain divided—so long as the idea of unity remains only an idea or a secret conviction in the hearts of men. "The unity that reflects the union of the Father and the Son must become manifest on earth in the actual life of the Church, in its message and in its outward order in the mutual relations of its members and its united action in the world." [124]

As Bishop Newbigin repeatedly says: "So long as the Church is content to live for itself, to turn its back on the world and face inwards, it will

---

[119] W. A. Visser 't Hooft, *The Pressure of Our Common Calling*, (New York: Doubleday & Company, Inc., 1959), p. 23.

[120] Ephesians 4, Hebrews 3:1, II Peter 1:10, John 17, etc.

[121] Visser 't Hooft, *op. cit.*, p. 26.

[122] How does unity grow? John 17:16—19, Hebrews 3:1—2, Ephesians 4:1—16. The calling to unity in Christ, John 17:18—25, Ephesians 4:1—16, I Corinthians 10:16—18.

[123] Visser 't Hooft, *op. cit.*, p. 82.

[124] *Ibid.*, p. 83.

always find sufficient reasons for being disunited ... the moment the Church turns out to the world and begins to take seriously the responsibility to be Christ's embassy to the world, then disunity among the messengers becomes an intolerable anomaly." [125]

However, in spite of the great press toward Christian unity, there are several which handicap the ecumenical cause. Generally they come under the heading of (1) theological factors or (2) non-theological factors such as (a) fear of the loss of identity, (b) impatience, (c) indifference and inertia, (d) despair of any final success.

One thing is certain, there are no "get-union-quick" schemes for Christian unity available to us. [126]

Several things necessary to keep in mind as we face the concerns of the ecumenical movement today are suggested by Reinhold Niebuhr [127] and W. Norman Pittenger. [128]

Niebuhr says:

> The ecumenical movement does not try to establish one unified church with the power to convict this or that church of heresy. Rather it establishes a place of encounter in which we can instruct each other by bringing our cherished treasures of grace and where by allowing the criticism of our fellow Christians to aid us in separating the "precious from the vile" we may all draw closer together "by all coming closer to the truth in Christ."

Pittenger says:

> ... a "watered-down" or "reduced" Christianity has no importance for contemporary men and women and sometimes very little relation to the historical faith for which our fathers lived and died. (Too often today) ... the World goes on its way, the church goes its; the two do not meet ... Surely we do not wish to cast off the great Christian tenets of faith, but equally surely, we wish to make them our own by appropriating them freely and understanding them in the light of contemporary knowledge ... all truth is of God who himself is Truth ... (failure to see this) ... will only result in the dismissal of Christianity to the category of old, lovely, but absurd folklore.

The chief questions in debate today are not charting the areas of agreement or disagreement among Christians, but determining the nature of

---

[125] Lesslie Newbigin, *One Body, One Gospel, One World—The Christian Mission Today,* (New York: International Missionary Council, 1958).

[126] Wedel, *International Journal of Religious Education, November,* 1961, p. 6.

[127] Reinhold Niebuhr, "Our Dependence Is On God," *The Christian Century,* September 1, 1954.

[128] W. Norman Pittinger, "Wanted: A New Christian Modernism," *The Christian Century,* April 6, 1955.

48

the church, its ministry and sacraments, and the nature of the unity we are seeking. Very few debate the necessity of the call to unity. "As things now stand," Albert C. Outler says, "our existing disagreements on the doctrine of the church, ministry and sacraments are insoluble." [129] All progress toward solving the question of the kind of unity we need, organic union or a strengthening and broadening of the counciliar unity, depends upon our willingness to hear God's living Voice within and to be obedient to it as we develop a keen historical sense.

Following is a list of some of the specific and somewhat basic questions and issues facing the ecumenical movement today. [130]

(1) "Reflections on the Divisions of Christians" by J. Robert Nelson.
   (a) Of what truth or value is the kind of Christian faith that seems utterly incapable of effecting reconciliation and peace among its members?
   (b) How can any one denomination interpret the Gospel or exemplify the new life in Christ in a manner more distinctly adequate than the potential manner of the Church in its wholeness and unity?
   (c) In the increasingly impersonal society of mankind, how can the community of Christians become an immediately perceptible reality?
   (d) Will the churches of America find the will and the wisdom to manifest the unity that is now historically possible? (Especially since VaticanII).

(2) Four principal alternative views on the ideal unity of the church [131].
   (a) The unity of fellowship—a spiritual unity only.
   (b) The unity of mutual recognition—a free interchange of memberships and ministers and full intercommunion between churches.
   (c) The unity of association—in fellowship and cooperative action through adding to present councils the added feature of mutual recognition of all Christians.
   (d) The unity of complete corporate or organic union.

(3) General areas of ecumenical discussion today.
   (a) The nature of the unity we have.
   (b) The nature of the unity we seek.
   (c) The nature of the disunity we deplore.
   (d) The nature of the pluralism we must accept.

---

[129] Albert C. Cutler, *The Christian Tradition and the Unity We Seek,* (New York: Oxford University Press, 1957), p. 8.

[130] Much of this was gleaned from *Christianity and Crisis. A Christian Journal of Opinion,* Vol. XXI, No. 18, October 30, 1961, p. 181.

[131] Henry P. van Dusan, "Conciliar Ecumenicity and Church Union," *Christianity and Crisis,* October 30, 1961, p. 188.

(4) The Problem of Communication.

    (a) How to proclaim with effectiveness the insights gained from ecumenical assemblies to the people in the churches in terms they will understand and with the same sense of urgency characteristic of the assemblies.

    (b) All ecumenical problems have to be worked out, ultimately, at the grass roots level in every local situation. The Christian layman is tremendously important in the ecumenical movement.

    (c) There is much need for a kind of conventicle movement within every local church in order for the churches to regain a sense of spiritual power in our society. Whenever a small group of Christians meet together for the purpose of sincere worship and study who are honestly striving to allow God to work in them through their daily lives, then the church is strong.

(5) Additional non-theological factors that must be considered.

    (a) The legacy of the Reformation (*i.e.,* separated churches centered in persons or in a particular system of procedure).

    (b) Methods of worship.

    (c) Differing ethical interpretations of social issues.

    (d) Social prestige.

    (e) Church and State issues.

    (f) Entire place of laity-clergy activities and responsibilities.

    (g) Brotherhood and coexistence in a pluralistic world, culture and society.

These, among others, are the major concerns of the ecumenical movement today. Slow, sometimes painful progress is being made on all fronts. Occasionally a minor set-back occurs but primarily the thrust of the movement has been and is presently in the direction of honest spiritual growth. There are no easy or simple solutions to any of these concerns but the "Stream of the Spirit" seems to be making its currents felt in every serious attempt to come to terms with these concerns. Of particular significance today is the work of those churches involved in COCU.

4. The Ecumenical Goal

> ... that they may be one; even as thou, Father, art in me, and I in thee, that they also may be in us, so that the world may believe that thou hast sent me. JOHN 17:21

As we contemplate the present world situation and see the vast political, sociological and technological changes and consider their effect upon the religious life of man we must never lose sight of the fact that this is God's creation. He has made us for a purpose and his purpose is sure to be successful. We live in a time of tremendous spiritual opportunity as well as in a time of hideous physical destruction with all its demoralizing effects. "The true alternative to an atomic holocaust is a world-wide awakening under the Holy Spirit." [132]

This is the dream of the ecumenical movement. This is the ideal toward which the religion Jesus brought to man moves. It is quite apparent that the leaders of this "great new fact of our time," the World Council of Churches, are sincere, dedicated, spiritually awakened men and women. [133]

The goal of the great majority of these dedicated leaders is not for fame or a super-church but is to seek ways of meeting the need for experiential-spiritual religion in our day through a reformation of the people so that the trends, necessarily begun four hundred years ago, may be reversed and the growth of the Christian Church may bring it closer to maturity instead of to ever wider disunity.

"The church exists to draw men to Christ—not to some dynamic leader, not to a doctrinal system, not to a form of government, not to a special interpretation of Scripture or sacraments." [134] The Ecumenical Movement is moving, slowly but definitely, toward this purpose of the Church and it seeks to point in the direction of this goal for all who take the time to look and to hear and to see with understanding love.

---

[132] Shoemaker, *op. cit.,* p. 55.

[133] The writer has participated in ecumenical endeavors since his college years and has had first-hand experience on the local state, and national levels. He has attended many ecumenical seminars and conferences in connection with National and World Council activities since his ordination. He has read literature in this entire field, and has held various official positions in ecumenical organizations. From all points of contact with the ecumenical movement and many of its leaders, he is convinced that this is part of a great new reformation of the church which is really only a continuation of the ideals of all the 16h century reformers when they first set out on their course of reformation.

[134] Samuel McCrea Cavert, *On the Road to Christian Unity,* (New York: Harper & Bros., 1961) p. 153.

CHAPTER V

SCHWENCKFELD AND THE ECUMENICAL IDEAL

1. Summary of the Basic Tenets of Schwenckfeld

*I*t is my conviction that Caspar Schwenckfeld sought to answer the
call to unity and used many of the methods that are now being used in
the ecumenical movement. Schwenckfeld maintained that a genuine reformation of the church is not the work of man but of God through
Christ in the Holy Spirit working in man. Required for such a reformation is a pure biblical knowledge of Christ that is experienced in life which
results in the unity of faith and also the freedom of expression, discussion and honest differences in non-essentials. This reformation is to be a
gradual process and is not to be based upon compulsory adherence to
man-made creeds and organizations or on "strained theological theories"
for the sake of concord. Rather, it is to be built on the knowledge of Christ,
the spiritual interpretation of Scripture, on freedom of conscience, on
faith and the fellowship of love. The principles of Christian love,
brotherhood, liberty, unity of purpose and experiential-spiritual religion
for which Caspar Schwenckfeld stood are eternally true. Rufus Jones
says: "There can be no question that the current of Christian thought
has been strongly setting in the direction which the spiritual reformers
took." [135]

The following are the basic tenets of the Reformation of the "Middle
Way" as carried on by Caspar Schwenckfeld and the "Confessors to the
Glory of Christ," in their search for peace and harmony among all God's
children in the "new community"—*i.e.*, the Church. [136]

---

[135] Jones, *op. cit.*, p. li.
[136] *CS.*, I, Intro., p. xvii—xliv.

52

a) Individualism. Schwenckfeld maintained that he must think for himself and so must every man. He must act for himself, no one can do what he ought to do. The more an individual makes of himself the better he can help his fellow men. Every person must be trained to think clearly and act responsively to the will of God. Each person is responsible for himself in the sight of God. The best developed persons are the most efficient parts of the social structure. Conformity, either voluntary or compulsory, was abhorrent to Schwenckfeld if it was not the result of personal conviction, arrived at by individual decision. Birth is individual, rebirth must also be individual.

b) Fundamental rights of the laity. Schwenckfeld himself was a layman and therefore was deeply concerned that all laymen have rights based upon the knowledge of what men are and what God would have them be. His reforming activity was based upon human rights and brotherhood of all God's children through Christ. As a nobleman he was able to care for the needs of all and he treated all classes of people as worthy children of the same God. He not only talked about the priesthood of all believers, he actually lived it and encouraged others to do the same. Fraternal law and democratic ideals were starting points from which the church could make visible its unity in Christ.

c) Christian liberty. He practiced tolerance, the freedom of debate, and recognized the rights of others in a very intolerable and intolerant age. He desperately tried to teach how coercion and force, creeds and dogmas never made Christians, they only make hypocrites. He stood for the freedom of individuals to think and to act according to a disciplined conscience. This, too, is a necessary starting point for the reformation of the church for it enables the transformation to move from within outward—from persons to institutions. Christ is the truth who makes us free. When he rules and lives within the individual, unity and love prevail among individuals.

d) Brotherhood. Christianity does not denounce humanity but rather seeks to purify it and bring it to perfection according to the love of God for all his children. God so loved the world that he gave his Son for the world. He is the regenerator of humanity and not the destroyer of its unity or its basic family relationships in the family of man. While the other leaders of the reformation thought primarily in terns of their own people, race, group, nation, etc., and sought to make others conform to their views, Schwenckfeld thought in terms of the whole human race.

e) The right of religious assembly. Where two or three are gathered in Christ's name, there is the Church. He believed in the right of small groups, whether led by a priest or minister or not, to meet together in conventicles for worship, study, prayer and conferences. He believed the *ecclesiola in ecclesia* held the very life blood of the kingdom of God. Without such study groups the church tends to become just another organization with the spirituality drained out. The conventicles of Schwenckfeld sought to keep the church from becoming simply a machine or a mass of external forms.

f) The Spirit above the letter. For Schwenckfeld, literalism was the way of bondage and death to Christianity. Experience and experiment are the true ways to religious progress. Christian faith rests upon the indwelling of Christ. He illuminates and reveals directly to the honest and sincere seeker after truth who searches the Scriptures for the truth that is in them. He always remembered that the actual event comes before anything is written about the event. Christ is active in history and in the believer and will lead into truth. Confessions of faith cannot take the place of the Bible and Scripture cannot take the place of the living Word, Jesus Christ. Schwenckfeld placed more emphasis upon the Holy Spirit than any of his contemporaries and it is plain to see that modern Christianity is beginning to deal more seriously with this whole area of the faith. Spirit above the ossified letter is basic to the unity of the church. At all times Schwenckfeld put the accent upon simplicity for the proper adornment of the Spirit. He was convinced God could and would and has spoken to the soul of man without external agencies. He thought that of all dead things a Spiritless congregation was the most deplorable. Schwenckfeld believed in the Holy Spirit because he was conscious of the guidance, teaching, comfort and sustaining presence of that Spirit of Truth throughout his life.

g) Character is above everything else in life. Schwenckfeld believed that only the Christian man, the one who obeys the leading of the Holy Spirit within, can preach or serve God well. There can be no real piety or Christian living without constant and conscious growth in Christian virtues. The Christian life is to make a difference in the way one lives and that difference must show upon the neighbor's welfare. Schwenckfeld was in favor of strict discipline among those who professed to be members of Christ's Church. One's beliefs must be expressed by the way one conducts his life. Faith without works is dead but so is the reverse true. Men must consider each other on the basis of character.

h) Unity of purpose not necessarily uniformity of organization or of mind. "If the Christian Church is a body of believers in Christ, then the fraternal bond is the first human thought and the first human act to be considered, and its maintenance is priceless, its goal is the embrace of the race in its ample and fostering arms."[137] That we love one another is the primary mark of a Christian and is the basis for unity in the Church. He held that Christians should be brothers, however variant their theological explanations might be. He was ready to associate with all who believed in Christ and behaved like Christians. He said, (p. 18 Course of Study) "I am most concerned that I be a member of the Church of God to which belong all those in all lands wherever they may be, who sincerely serve and worship God, whether or not they belong to any one confession of faith or order of worship." His hope was for a truly ecumenical church, one that really believes in and practices the brotherhood of man in Christ as well as talks about it. Therefore he worked for the transformation of individual lives from which he sincerely believed a truly free, united Christian Church would develop. The divisions among the churches were caused, he thought, by the insistence upon the external superficialities and upon a literal interpretation of scripture. He insisted that it was through a spiritual oneness with God through faith, which is conscious surrender to God, daily fellowship with God, and participation in the divine nature through Christ and the power of the Holy Spirit that Christian unity can be achieved. As he would not allow anyone to coerce his conscience, so he refrained from the use of force in teaching his ideas. Again he said,

> I would rather die ten deaths than join churches that on account of their statutes and articles of faith, contrary to the example of Christ, burn, hang, drown or in some other way persecute God-fearing and pious men who accept Christ but do not happen to accept their particular creed.

i) Education of the conscience. Schwenckfeld always stressed education for the purpose of raising ethical standards among the people. He

---

[137] *Ibid.*, I, xxxix

was aware, of course, that only by conversion and the indwelling of Christ could men live righteously, but he did not neglect the fact that the outer man had to be educated in order to point to inner realities. For Schwenckfeld, the conscience directed and cultured by the Spirit of Christ was the most important part of personality. The proper education of the conscience is important for the Christian Life. To make Christ really known would lead to greater Christian unity.

j) Speculative philosophy has no part in the construction of sound Christian thought. For Schwenckfeld, the Bible plus positive Christian experience, plus inner direction by the Holy Spirit, furnished the basis for Christian thought. He believed man's reason was infected by the Fall and needed conversion, too. It could not be relied upon, unaided by the Spirit, experience and Scripture. He held that only those who were born anew and had deep Christian experience, both inner and outer, and who relied upon the Holy Spirit were capable of understanding the Bible and of teaching or preaching in the household of God.

k) The Gospel must be applied to the needs of society. Schwenckfeld practiced the best elements of the Social Gospel in his very life. His own life was a kind of experimental sociology conducted according to the prescriptions of Christ. He encouraged all people, especially the nobility who were more able, to meet the welfare needs of society in the name of Christ. This, too, was basic to his ideal for a united Church and for the program of his reformation.

2. Summary of the Dominant Concerns of Schwenckfeld

Upon the above tenets Schwenckfeld based his religious activity and hopes for a united Church. In the light of these, let us take a summary look at some of his dominant concerns:

a) Practical theology. The guiding motivation of Schwenckfeld was his concern for a practical ethical Christianity. He lamented the fact that the Lutheran Reformation was making little or no change in the morality of the people. He saw that this was true of all the movements which stressed literalism and externals. Therefore, he endeavored to stimulate a reformation that would change lives as well as beliefs.

Dr. Maier clearly indicates that this practical theology of the Middle Way is seen in various tensions of the Reformation Era—(1) In faith-works tension Schwenckfeld took his stand between Roman Catholicism's rigid morality and Lutheranism's lack of ethical thrust. Schwenckfeld emphasized a faith-works synthesis. (2) In the controversy over free will, Schwenckfeld stood between Luther and Erasmus. He claimed sinful man is not free to do good but the Christian man is free. (3) In the discussions about predestination he again took to middle ground, saying man is never predestined to eternal damnation. He leaned toward a type of predestination of the believer but chided the Swiss for seeming to make it central in their system. (4) In the Eucharistic and Baptism battles, Schwenckfeld again seems to have been midway between Luther and Zwingli, and, Luther and the Anabaptists.

In all of this, Schwenckfeld's emphasis was on the practical level as opposed to the purely theoretical level.

b) Inner and Outer Word. There is a fundamental dualism in all of Schwenckfeld's thinking—an internal and an external essence to everything.[138] The two realms are independent of each other and there is no necessary correlation between them. This appears to be the key to understanding his theology. He constantly and consistently emphasizes the importance of the inner realm with its immediate communication between Christ and the Christian. It is important to note, however, he never got carried away with this type of thinking as some of the more fanatical spiritualists have been known to do.

It was his Christology that influenced his thinking on all other aspects of Christianity. The Word of God is spirit and life (John 6) and therefore it is Christ himself. The Bible, the external letter, is "word of God" only in a derived sense. In the same way the sermon, symbols, pictures, sacraments, etc., can all be "words of God" but never the Word, which is Christ. The inner Word is not conveyed by external means. The outer word simply points toward or declares or announces the inner Word.

Thus, the Bible is considered to be inspired by the Holy Spirit, innerrant[139] and normative for Christian faith and life.[140] But we cannot refer to the Bible as The Word of God. It is simply the written record of the voice of God as heard by and sifted through men of faith.

---

[138] *Ibid.*, II, 454, 307, 354 ff., 404, 468, 485; III, 113, 176; IV, 549; V, 66—69; VII, 188; IX, 113; X, 292; XV, 12—15.

[139] *Ibid.*, IV, 107.

[140] *Ibid.*, III, 679, XII, 426, 451; S. Schultz, *op. cit.*, chap. 20.

Schwenckfeld was an ardent Bible student and used it continuously as an inspired book of devotion, inspiration and instruction. But, he was always firm in stating that it is not the inner Word, it is part of the outer "word of God." The inner Word, Christ, helps us to interpret the outer word correctly.

c) The Sacraments. Schwenckfeld's relations with the Anabaptists grew increasingly worse even though Luther *et al.* accused him of being one of them. He never accepted the charge for he considered the Anabaptists to be too legalistic, too intolerant und too ignorant of the depths of spiritual religion.[141]

He also could not agree with Luther's *ex opere operato* interpretations of the sacraments. However, Schwenckfeld did not want to throw out the external observances so long as the spiritual reality was accepted. He had no argument with the use of externals as such in religion. What he did not condone was the use of externals in place of, or to bring about, the spiritual reality.

The sixth chapter of John forms the basis for his understanding of the Eucharist. He taught that Jesus spoke a parable at the last supper, using bread and wine to represent himself—"My body is this, namely a bread; My blood is this, namely a cup or a drink." He who is not born of God cannot commune with God no matter how many external observances he attends. Judas is the example for this. The Eucharist was instituted for those who are already Christians, it does not impart grace. The external observance is a memorial—"this do in remembrance" but the Christian spiritually feeds upon the risen Lord every day for He is always "really-spiritually present" to the believer.[142] Schwenckfeld recommended a *Stillstand* until all would unite in a spiritual understanding of the Supper. He did not intend this to be a permanent practice for he valued the external observance. However, for him the inward communion is the most important and the *Stillstand* became a kind of trademark of the Middle Way until 1877.

Schwenckfeld's teaching on Baptism is similar to that of the Lord's Supper. While believing in "Believer's Baptism" he did not insist on rebaptism as the Anabaptists were doing. External baptism does not wash away sin, it can merely call attention to the spiritual. The inward spirit-

---

[141] *CS.*, VIII, 865—868.   [142] *Ibid.*, VIII, 228.

ual baptism must take place before the outer has any real value. He taught there is no scriptural grounds for infant baptism. He said, "I regard the baptism of infants to be the beginning of papistry and the foundation of all error and ignorance in the church of Christ and moreover, the destruction of all piety and . . . the apostolic ministry. I am not able to think otherwise, with a good conscience, until I shall have been better informed from the scriptures."[143] He himself had been baptized as an infant and never accepted rebaptism because, as he said, that sufficed so far as the external rite is concerned.[144] He never encouraged infant baptism for salvation is not dependent on any external ceremony, time or age, but on Jesus Christ. Outward baptism, then, is for those born of God, who promise to walk in the obedience of faith. He always insisted that instruction precede the celebration of every outward observance of the sacraments.

d) The Church and Ministry. Schwenckfeld believed there is an internal and an external Church. The internal Church is the true, universal body of Christ made up of all who by faith have been reborn and have Christ living in them. The external church is the one we see with all its organizations and activities and it includes both believers and hypocrites. Salvation does not depend upon membership in the external church, but it means acceptance of the internal Church. His general attitude toward the institutional churches varies because he was always more interested in inward religion than in the precise form it took.

However, he was deeply concerned about the unity of Christ's body on earth. He believed the true Church of Christ pre-dated the historical event of Christ for all God's people of faith are members of it. He is the same to faith yesterday, today and forever. "Before Abraham was, I am," said Christ. Actually, the covenant of Grace antedated the covenant of the law by the very nature of faith (Hebrews 11). Therefore, the promises concerning Christ and his church are to be accepted in the spirit and nature of faith and are not to be limited by time and history. Jesus also said: "I came not to abolish but to fulfill." The true Church, for Schwenckfeld, is not built or governed or changed by man. It is built by Christ alone and love is its most distinguishing mark. Amidst diversity of knowledge, practices and specific beliefs, all may be one in spirit and purpose through love. Only "in Christ" and "through Christ" can the

---

[143] *Ibid.*, III, 858.   [144] *Ibid.*, VII, 69.

ecumenical church be realized in its external form. Schwenckfeld said where there is genuine Christian love there is no occasion for anxiety about Christian unity. However good and desirable external organizational unity may be, Christian brotherly love and unity do not necessarily require organic union. Basic Christian unity, for Schwenckfeld, is not to be found in external things, appearances or ceremonies, but inwardly in unity of hearts which are of one mind, one will and one soul in Christ, the only Mediator and Unifier of God and man. [145]

It was Schwenckfeld's cherished hope that there might be one united Christian Church. Recognizing human differences, he insisted this can come only by God through spiritual means. He remains a challenge to all honest searchers for the truth about the failure of the reformation to bring about the ecumenical church. [146]

In reference to the ministry of the external church, Schwenckfeld again stresses the truth that the real ministry is that of Christ Himself who speaks directly to the heart, mind and soul. He never rejected the office of the ministry and held that it was necessary for instruction, reproof and guidance for the outer man.

God uses his servants, the ministers, the Bible, the sacraments, the churches, etc., for the instruction of the outer man that he may walk uprightly and be prepared to live according to the will of God after the inner man hears and responds to the inner Word. The function of the externals is merely to call attention to the inward. The state or civil authorities have no jurisdiction over spiritual concerns and the external church should avoid intermingling with the functions of the state. The state was ordained by God to conduct and provide an orderly society, it has no right to interfere or to influence religious convictions. Civil obedience is always required by the Christian except where the Christian conscience cannot honestly obey. Obedience to God must always come first. Therefore, the Church and the State should remain separate.

e) The Question of Abraham. The ecumenical ideal as reflected in Schwenckfeld finds expression in his interpretation of the faith of Abraham. Abraham heard the voice of God and did as he was told. [147]

---

[145] S. Schultz, *Course of Study ...*, p. 77.   [146] *Ibid.*, p. 9.

[147] In chaps. 5 and 6 *Knight of Faith*, Dr. Sayppel makes a very dramatic and challenging presentation of Kierkegaard's "theological suspension of the ethical" in *Fear and Trembling* and relates this to Schwenckfeld as the Knight of Faith.

Abraham was ready to sacrifice his own son because he had heard God's Word and because he had faith in God. Both Schwenckfeld and Kierkegaard saw in the Jewish patriarch a central figure of Christian religion.[148] Abraham was one of the first to be spiritually reborn in the non-creaturely Christ for "Before Abraham was, I am." Abraham, and all men of faith, "in the stream of the Spirit" are members of the ecumenical Church.

However, who can say: God has spoken to me? Who can honestly say they are responding to the voice of the inner Word today? The person who hears and obeys that Word is a lonely, exceptional man as was Abraham before the altar with his son lying before him, as was Schwenckfeld, alone before all forces seeking to draw him away from the "stream of the Spirit," as was Kierkegaard, as was Christ on the cross. Schwenckfeld maintained that to the Christian God is real, he speaks, he must be obeyed. Therefore, the Christian is one who obeys God regardless of consequences.

It appears that if the Ecumenical Ideal is to become a reality, the question of the faith of Abraham must be considered and taken very seriously. The Church of Jesus Christ is one in him! But the churches must be willing to surrender themselves totally to God's will for unity in love and faith or there can be no outward form of unity that can be lasting. Until individuals first are willing to surrender to God *in toto,* the institutional churches will not, and in fact cannot unite. As Schwenckfeld lived what he believed, so we must seek to live. As he condemned static orthodox churches with their outward show of religiosity but a lack of spiritual depth and understanding, so we today must call for an inwardness of religion that expresses itself in the unity of love and the bond of peace in obedience to our Lord's prayer in John 17. Either we follow Christ or we perish. There can be no other alternative in the kind of world in which we live today.

---

[148] Seyppel, *op. cit.,* p. 138.

CONCLUSIONS

I. The Place of Schwenckfeld in the Church

Schwenckfeld's "middle" position among the Reformers offers insight into the causes and meaning of the deep divisions of the church that marked Western Europe in the sixteenth century and which marks modern Protestantism today. It also points in the direction toward which the dreams of a united church may come to the experiential level of life. Caspar Schwenckfeld von Ossig certainly was a mediating person who stood above party and creed and church and placed Christ at the center around whom his children could find their oneness. [149]

The question is asked, Why did his reformation fail? The answer is to be found partly in the fact that in the entire history of man, wise counsel and wise men have been spurned by those in authority to the detriment of the common good of many. Personal ambition, egotism and power have little time for anything or anyone who threatens their present status. Schwenckfeld definitely was a threat to the *status quo* and to orthodox literalism in the church. He was "superbly out of date" and was not understood by even the great of his day because they were concerned with the immediate situation at hand.

But, as we ponder the question more deeply, why did his reformation fail?, we begin to realize that actually it has not failed. It is still in process. The modern ecumenical movement seems to be a part of this continuing reformation. He sought a reformation from within, one that

---

[149] "Caspar Schwenckfeld, in his vision of the universal church, was clearly the heir of a great and richly complex tradition—classical, biblical, patristic, mystical. His was the vision of a universal church embracing the righteous faithful in all climes and times; his was the vision of the universal, peaceloving, serving and saving church of the everreigning Christ the King of Grace."—Dr. George H. Williams, address December 10, 1961, 400th Anniversary Service commemorating the death of Caspar Schwenckfeld, Central Schwenkfelder Church, Worcester, Pa.

takes time and patience and much leaning upon the guidance and power of the Holy Spirit. Dr. Battles reminds us,

> Christian history has a way of throwing up the rejected good of a past era to the immense enrichment of a later time ... Is not this 400th Anniversary of Schwenckfeld's death and celebration of the completion of the *Corpus* of his works the signal for us ... to listen to his counsels and to apply them boldly and creatively to our own troubled time?" [150]

In his ministry and life Schwenckfeld lived the ecumenical ideal and called upon everyone to place Christ and his spirit above the killing letter so that a living fellowship of committed Christians could bear witness to the world of God's great love and concern for his people. Such a fellowship would truly be united as "Confessors to the Glory of Christ." He worked not to found a church, a denomination, or to gain a following for himself. But, by his work he has found a most significant place in the history of the Church. He has helped to keep the churches closer to the "stream of the Spirit" which maintains the true unity of Christ's Body.

It would seem, therefore, in the light of the dominant concerns of the ecumenical movement as outlined in Chapter IV and the relation of Schwenckfeld to the ecumenical ideal in Chapter V, that Caspar Schwenckfeld has most to say in the area of strengthening the conciliar movements with emphasis upon mutual recognition of all Christians.

2. The Primary Contribution of the Schwenkfelder Church to the Ecumenical Movement

Observers of the world situation today, whether they speak from within or without the church, seem to agree that the world must develop a sense of community or perish through its own divisiveness. We cannot deny that our world is divided into at least two armed camps and that with each new scientific development comes an increased ability to destroy ourselves. We live in a pluralistic society in a pluralistic world.

---

[150] Dr. Ford L. Battles in a sermon delivered at the Central Schwenkfelder Church, December 10, 1961. Dr. Battles points out that Schwenckfeld "lives on in his books, but only if his books are read" and, we should add, followed seriously. "But his own books drive us back to *the* Book and *the* Book in turn leads us to Jesus Christ the living Word of God. If those Christians who now bear Schwenckfeld's name fail to trace for themselves the path that led Schwenckfeld to his Master, they have no reason for a continued existence."

What has the Church of Jesus Christ to say to this kind of world? What has the Schwenkfelder Church to say to the Church?

Because of the constant flux and the resultant anxieties of our time, the churches are beginning to become aware of the need to recognize religion as being inward and yet, at the same time, practical, expressing itself in outward deeds of love. There seems to be a growing awareness of the strengths of the experiential-spiritual tradition and of its historical thread going back to Jesus himself. This spiritual thread goes even to Abraham and before through the eternal Christ.

But, to the vast majority of people such things are still out of date. Most people in our day are followers of what has been called simply "Religion in General," [151] which is characterized by a simple interest in and an attitude in favor of anything that faintly sounds like it might be religious. This religious attitude which seems so popular today has no pope or president or formal dogma. It lacks a name, but it includes elements of secularism, naturalism, nationalism and humanism. It avoids the necessity of definite decision and is extremely broad-minded and tolerant. It is not Christ centered and therefore not basically Christian. Yet it passes for Christianity in the minds of many within the institutional churches today. It takes its standards from society and measures its successes in terms of the size of the treasury, the rate of increase in members, and the variety of program in terms of number and activity, without regard for the quality or the content of the activity. This kind of religious attitude is the popular, prevalent thing in America today and because of it, Christianity seems irrelevant to many people. Because of this, the religion of Schwenckfeld appears to be the kind of religion needed today.

As Christians we must take care not to put greater value on what we do for God than on what he does for us. The religion of Schwenckfeld places God in his rightful position and condemns those churches and ministers who tend to call attention to themselves and to the tremendous amount of work they do instead of calling attention to what God has done for us in Jesus Christ. The religion of Schwenckfeld places much emphasis upon individual responsibility to God for the welfare of all men.

---

[151] Martin E. Marty, *The New Shape of American Religion*, (New York: Harper & Brothers, 1959).

64

The Church must constantly call the world to recognize the truth of St. Augustine's statement: "If we have God we have all and without Him we have nothing." Caspar Schwenckfeld's motto was very similar: "Nil Triste Christo Recepto," (Having Christ, I am not sad). There is always imminent danger facing the churches whenever they become too much concerned about the outward and neglect the inward. To be concerned about both, while giving priority to the inward, was Schwenckfeld's genius and can be the greatest contribution of the Schwenkfelder Church to modern ecumenical discussions.

The Schwenkfelder church may be out of date, but it can be "superbly out of date" if it remains true to the insights of Caspar Schwenckfeld von Ossig.

What responsibility rests upon the 2,500 Schwenkfelders who comprise the five congregations of Schwenkfelder descendants today?

First—They must recognize that the Church of Jesus Christ cannot be known or seen from the outside. One has to get inside to really be creatively alive. One has to become involved. He has to have a direct, personal encounter with God here and now. It is not enough simply to stand in the reflected light of a great heritage. One must seriously ask: Is this heritage ending or is it being continued through me? Am I helping to reflect the Light of the World who illuminated Caspar Schwenckfeld?

Second—As Schwenckfeld attempted to be the physician of a dissected church in his day, so his followers need to become a healing force in the divided church of today wherever they may live. They must be engaged in all ecumenical concerns, recognizing that mere outward unity is not enough.

Third—As Schwenckfeld remained a layman and spoke with prophetic voice to the clergy of his day, so all his followers today must re-examine the meaning of the "priesthood of all believers" and become intelligently concerned about the unity of Christ's Church by witnessing to it and working for it no matter what they do to "earn their living."

Fourth—As Schwenckfeld saw that the need of his day was to rededicate the outward church to the depth of spiritual reality and thus became a great leader in showing the way to unity in Christ by helping to educate and raise up valiant leaders, so the Schwenkfelder Church of today must raise up leaders from within its own ranks and must make its people aware of its profound spiritual heritage so that the cause of Christ may continue in unbroken line.

Fifth—As Schwenckfeld would not compromise spiritual truth for the sake of mere outward peace and concord, so the Schwenkfelder church of today must guard against a too easy compromise of its tradition for mere convenience. Church merger may well be the next step for the Schwenkfelder church, but this must be carefully studied and prayerfully derived.

Sixth—As Schwenckfeld allowed the Holy Spirit to guide him through the Scriptures to the living Word of God, Jesus Christ, so the Schwenkfelder Church must direct its people to the same Word who alone can give life meaning and purpose. The Schwenkfelder Church must re-emphasize the "conventicle" method of serious Bible study, discussion and prayer.

Seventh—As Schwenckfeld sought to avoid coercion, so the Schwenkfelder people must avoid being imprisoned by their traditions and must sincerely and honestly seek to learn from their tradition how to make new application of spiritual truths to the conditions of today.

The basic task of The Schwenkfelder Church, as of all churches, is to seek for an experiential-spiritual religion which will enable its members to translate the Christian Faith from the first century through the mill of history, by way of the sixteenth century, to the present ecumenical movement in order to inspire the world to become the Household of God. Schwenckfeld gave no blueprint for the ecumenical church, but he did direct us to the only source of Christian unity—Jesus Christ.

Caspar Schwenckfeld von Ossig, 1489—1561, was a Christian noble-man and truly a "Confessor of the Glory of Christ" seeking the unity of his Church. He was "superbly out of date." We must not forget, however, that no one man or institution possesses the whole truth. Man's hope today is, as was affirmed by the early Christians as well as by Schwenck-feld, in simply belonging to the way Christ gave us. What matters most is that the individual seeker of truth should seek honestly for life's meaning and life's source in Christ.

BIBLIOGRAPHY

BOOKS

PRIMARY SOURCE

Corpus Schwenckfeldianorum. Vols. I—XIX, Leipzig: Breitkopf and Härtel, 1907—1961.

Published under the auspices of the Schwenkfelder Church and the Hartford Theological Seminary. Volumes I to XV contain his writings from 1521 to 1557. Volume XVI contains his writings from 1558 to 1561. Volumes XVII to XVIII contain miscellaneous documents throughout the span of Schwenckfeld's literary activity which were not included in Volumes I to XVI. Volume XIX contains a topical index to the entire work, compiled by Selina G. Schultz. This monumental work was brought to completion in the 400th Anniversary Year of Schwenckfeld's death.

SECONDARY SOURCES ON SCHWENCKFELD

Jones, Rufus M. *Spiritual Reformers in the 16th and 17th Centuries.* Boston: Beacon Press, 1914.

Kriebel, Howard W. *The Schwenkfelders in Pennsylvania.* Lancaster, Pa.: The New Era Printing Company, 1904.

Reprinted from Vol. XIII, proceedings of the Pennsylvania German Society.

Maier, Paul L. *Caspar Schwenckfeld on the Person and Work of Christ.* The Netherlands: Royal Van Gorcum Ltd. Assen, 1959.

Schultz, Christopher. *A Vindication of Caspar Schwenckfeld von Ossig.* Allentown, Pa.: Schlechter, 1942.

Translated and edited by Elmer Schultz Gerhard and printed for the Board of Publication of the Schwenkfelder Church. Original "Erlauterung für herrn Caspar Schwenckfeld" was written in 1771.

Schultz, Selina G. *Caspar Schwenckfeld von Ossig: Spiritual Interpreter of Christianity. Apostle of the Middle Way, Pioneer in Modern Religious Thought.* Philadelphia: Walther Printing House, 1947.

—, *A. Course of Study in the Life and Teachings of Caspar Schwenckfeld von Ossig (1489—1561) and the History of the Schwenkfelder Religious Movement (1518—1958).* Pennsburg, Pa.: Board of Publication of the Schwenkfelder Church, 1959.

Seyppel, Joachim H. *Schwenckfeld: Knight of Faith.* Pennsburg, Pa.: The Schwenkfelder Library, 1961.

Wach, Joachim. *Types of Religious Experience: Christian and Non-Christian.* Chicago: University of Chicago Press, 1951.

SOURCES ON THE REFORMATION ERA

Althaus, Paul. *Zur Charakteristik der evangelischen Gebetslitteratur im Reformations-jahrhundert*. Leipzig: 1914.

Bainton, Roland H. *Here I Stand*. New York: Abingdon Press, 1950.

Friedmann, Robert. *Mennonite Piety Through the Centuries*. Goshen: 1949.

Grimm, Harold J. *The Reformation Era 1500—1650*. New York: The Macmillan Company, 1954.

Henssi, Karl. *Kompendium der Kirchengeschichte. Siebente Auflage*. Tübingen: 1930.

Huizinga, Johan. *Erasmus and the Age of Reformation*. New York: Harper Torch-book, 1957.

Latourette, K. S. *A History of Christianity*. New York: Harper and Brothers, 1953.

Phillips, Margaret Mann. *Erasmus and the Northern Renaissance*. New York: The Macmillan Company, 1950.

Spinka, Matthew. *Advocates of Reform*. Philadelphia: The Westminster Press, 1953.

Stevenson, William. *The Story of the Reformation*. Richmond, Va.: John Knox Press, 1959.

SOURCES ON THE ECUMENICAL MOVEMENT AND GENERAL INFORMATION

Brown, Robert McAfee. *The Spirit of Protestantism*. New York: Oxford University Press, 1961.

Cavert, Samuel McCrea. *On the Road to Christian Unity*. New York: Harper & Bros., 1961.

Garrison, W. E. *The Quest and Character of a United Church*. New York: Abingdon Press, 1957.

Goodall, Norman. *The Ecumenical Movement: What It Is and What It Does*. New York: Oxford University Press, 1961.

Harner, Nevin C. *I Believe*. Philadelphia: The Christian Education Press, 1954.

Hunt, George L. *A Guide to Christian Unity*. St. Louis: The Bethany Press, 1958.

Latourette, K. S. *The Emergence of a World Christian Community*. New Haven: Yale University Press, 1949.

Marty, Martin E. *The New Shape of American Religion*. New York: Harper & Brothers, 1959.

Morrison, Charles C. *Can Protestantism Win America?*. New York: Harper & Brothers, 1948.

—, *The Unfinished Reformation*. New York: Harper & Brothers, 1953.

Munro, W. Fraser. *Roman Catholic Tradition and the Protestant Faith*. Nashville, Tenn.: Tidings, 1959.

Newbigin, Lesslie. *The Household of God*. New York: Friendship Press, 1954.

—, *One Body. One Gospel. One World—The Christian Mission Today*. New York: International Missionary Council, 1958.

Outler, Albert C. *The Christian Tradition and the Unity we Seek*. New York: Oxford University Press, 1957.

Rouse and Neill. *A History of the Ecumenical Movement 1517—1948*. Philadelphia: Westminster Press, 1954.

Shoemaker, Samuel M. *With the Holy Spirit and With Fire.* New York: Harper & Brothers, 1960.

Visser 't Hooft, W. A. *The Pressure of Our Common Calling.* New York: Doubleday & Company, Inc., 1959.

Whale, J. S. *The Protestant Tradition.* Cambridge: University Press, 1955.

ARTICLES AND PERIODICALS

"A Message to the Churches in the Commonwealth of Pennsylvania," from the Pennsylvania Council of Churches, 1962.

Bailey, Roland. "What is Existentialism? The Creed of Commitment and Action," London: S.P.C.K., 1950.

Bradley, William L. "The Theology of the Holy Spirit," *The Bulletin of the Hartford Seminary Foundation*, No. 24, June, 1958.

Christianity and Crisis. A Christian Journal of Opinion. Vol. XXI, No. 18. Special issue on "Christian Unity," October 30, 1961.

Evanston Notebook. Published by the committee on "interpretation and support of the United States Conference of the World Council of Churches," New York: 1954.

International Journal of Religious Education. An official publication of the Division of Christian Education, National Council of Churches. Special Issue on "The Church is One," November, 1961.

Lord, John Wesley. "Is Christ Divided?" Address at the 50th Anniversary Service of the Pennsylvania Council of Churches, Harrisburg, Pa., November 7, 1961.

Lowell, G. Stanley. "The Sin of Separation," *Liberty: A Magazine of Religious Freedom.* ed. Roland R. Hegstad, Washington, D. C., January-February, 1962.

Maier, Paul L. "Caspar Schwenckfeld and the Schwenkfelders," an address given to the 76th Annual Meeting of the American Historical Association, December 22—30, 1961, Washington, D. C.

Newbigin, Lesslie. "The Urgency of the Gospel in Today's World," a message adopted by the Division of Foreign Missions of the National Council of Churches in Dayton, Ohio, December 4—7, 1955.

The Christian Century

May 12, 1954. "Nothing to Fear at Evanston," by Charles M. Crowe.
May 26, 1954. p. 62.
August 11, 1954. "The World Council Still Seeks Unity," by Angus Dun.
September 1, 1954. "Our Dependence Is On God," by Reinhold Niebuhr.
September 8, 1954. "The Gospel for this Generation," by C. W. Ranson.
September 15, 1954. "What Is the World Council?" by Kathleen Bliss.
September 15, 1954. "World Tensions and Unity in Christ," by Eivind Berggrav.
September 22, 1954. "Evanston 1954." (Special issue)
October 27, 1954. "Putting Up With the Church," by W. Norman Pittinger.
December 29, 1954. "The Pace of our Christian Witness," by George F. MacLeod.
January 5, 1955. "Evanston—An American Evaluation," by Robert L. Calhoun.
January 19, 1955. "Spiritual Lag in Today's World," by James McBride Dabbs.
March 23, 1955. "The Strategy of the Churches," by Eugene Carson Blake.
April 6, 1955. "Wanted: A New Christian Modernism," by W. Norman Pittinger.
February 29, 1956. "The Unity Christ Seekts," by Harold J. Ockenga.

March 14, 1956. "What Kind of Unity Do We Want?" by Kenneth T. Henderson.

March 21, 1956. "Toward a New Protestantism," by Walter F. Reif.

April 4, 1956. "Unity and Communication," by Richard R. Caemmerer.

June 13, 1956. "The Unity We Have," by Albert C. Outler.

July 10, 1957. "True and False Unity," by Walter Marshall Horton.

January 8, 1958. "Our Cooperative Witness to Our Oneness in Christ," by Truman B. Douglass.

July 30, 1958. "The Ecumenical Detour," by Charles C. Morrison.

March 9, 1960. "The Nature of Protestant Disuniy," by Charles C. Morrison.

June 1, 1960. "In Defense of Christian Pluralism," by Lloyd J. Averill.

February 8, 1961. "The Church and Unity," by Gerald Kennedy

February 15, 1961. "Prospectus for the Church," by Cecil Northcott.

June 14, 1961. "All in Each Place One," by James E. Wagner.

October 11, 1961. "For a World Christian Mission," by Alan Walker.

October 25, 1961. "The Task of Protestantism Today," by Warren Ashby.

November 22, 1961. "Who Belongs to Christ?" by J. Irwin Miller.

November 29, 1961. "The Road Ahead for the Church," by Deane W. Ferm.

December 20, 1961. "The Burden of the Christian," by Charles Malik.

January 10, 1962. "The New Delhi Assembly of the World Council of Churches." (specil issue)

The Mennonite. Published by the Board of Education and Publication of the General Conference of the Mennonite Church. A weekly magazine. Newton, Kansas. Special series of articles on the question of church unity.

October 24, 1961. "High Hopes for Unity," by William Keeney.

August 29, 1961. "Variety in the Early Church," by Vernon Neufeld.

January 2, 1962. "Mandate for Oneness," by William Klassen.

January 16, 1962. "Oneness Through the Spirit," by William Klassen.

February 6, 1962. "Origin of the Ecumenical Movement," by Russell L. Mast.

February 13, 1962. "The Nature of the Ecumenical Movement," by Russell L. Mast.

February 20, 1962. "Fulfilling the Ecumenical Movement," by Russell L. Mast.

The Schwenckfeldian. Published bi-monthly by the Board of Publication of the Schwenkfelder Church, Pennsburg, Pa. Those issues used for this thesis:

1956. June; September-October; November-December.

1957. July-August; September-October; November-December.

1958. January-February; March-April; September-October; November-December.

1959. March-April; May-June; July-August; September-October.

1960. September-October; November-December.

1961. September-October; November-December.

Van Dusen, Henry P. "The Spirit: A Time to Be Stern," Newsweek, December 14, 1959.

Wach, Joachim. "Casper Schwenckfeld, a Pupil and a Teacher in the School of Christ," The Journal of Religion. Vol. XXVI, No. 1. Chicago: The University of Chicago Press, January, 1946.

Wagner, James E. "Holding the World Together," a sermon delivered on the CBS Church of the Air, January 1, 1956.

Who Are the Schwenkfelders Selections from the Genealogical Record of the Schwenkfelder Families. Published by the Board of Publication of the Schwenkfelder Church, Pennsburg, Pa., 1923.

70